Flipping Good Pancakes

SUDI PIGOTT

PHOTOGRAPHY BY MAJA SMEND

KYLE BOOKS

TO MY TOTALLY INCREDIBLE AND STILL PANCAKE-LOVING SON THEO

An Hachette UK Company
www.hachette.co.uk

First published in Great Britain in 2017 by
Kyle Books, an imprint of Kyle Cathie Ltd
Carmelite House
50 Victoria Embankment
London EC4Y 0DZ
www.kylebooks.co.uk

This edition first published in 2018

ISBN 978 1 90948 791 8

Distributed in the US by Hachette Book Group,
1290 Avenue of the Americas, 4th and 5th Floors,
New York, NY 10104

Distributed in Canada by Canadian Manda Group,
664 Annette St., Toronto, Ontario, Canada M6S 2C8

Editor: Judith Hannam
Editorial Assistant: Hannah Coughlin
Copy Editor: Jan Cutler
Americanizer: Christy Lusiak
Designer: Nicky Collings
Photographer: Maja Smend
Illustrator: Ohn Mar Win
Food Stylist: Lizzie Harris
Prop Stylist: Tonia Shuttleworth
Production: Nic Jones and Gemma John

Printed and bound in China

10 9 8 7 6 5 4 3 2 1

Contents

Introduction

Who says pancakes should only be eaten with syrup and sugar? There is a world beyond for the gastronomically curious. Pancakes in all their delicious diversity have long been one of the most pleasurable, life-affirming parts of my culinary explorations, from the crisp outside, chewy within *cong you bing* I first discovered in Singapore, to chestnut flour *necci* in Tuscany. My friends call me "the pancake doyenne" as I always return from vacations relishing new recipes to expand my repertoire. But it's not just me: pancakes arouse equally enthusiastic feelings in others. I'd go as far as to say it's a truth universally consumed—we all love pancakes. They make us happy and the everyday special, and the ritual in the preparing, cooking, and flipping merely adds to their appeal. They can be both a quintessential comfort food and a decadent, intimate, even elegant treat. Most are easy to rustle up using a few, usually inexpensive, and infinitely versatile, savory or sweet ingredients, plus they're speedy to make, even if their perfection requires a little prowess. A few take longer, but that's usually resting time and the results are so rewarding.

Pancakes are much-loved as portable street food around the world. I treasure memories of my regular fix of creamy garlic mushroom-filled crêpes cooked to order at a stall after a long stroll on the Heath close to my first apartment in London. I recall waiting hungrily in line as the sound of the crêpe sizzling as it hit the pan made me drool in anticipation. Among my other favorites are the steaming hot, crunchy *socca* found in Nice. I also adore Columbian *arepas* and turmeric-laden, paper-thin rice flour and coconut milk Vietnamese *banh xeo* stuffed with crunchy vegetables. Almost every global culture has its pancake, and *Flipping Good Pancakes* contains recipes from more than 25 countries, from as-thin-as-one-dares French crêpes to lacy fermented South Indian dosa and exotically fragrant Arabic *atayef.*

What's more, pancakes are often associated with celebration and festival. Long before Shrove Tuesday, the final feast day when all good things have to be consumed before the start of Lent, pancakes were made to mark the end of winter and the beginning of spring. According to the pagan festival of Maslenitsa, the changes of the season were a struggle between Jarilo, the god of vegetation, fertility, and spring, and the evil spirits of cold, darkness, and winter. It was believed that to help vanquish winter and bring in spring, hot, round pancakes symbolizing the sun should be eaten to bring its warmth and power. In France, *la Chandeleur*, or Candlemas, is celebrated on February 2nd, and eating crêpes—usually filled with apple or cherries—is said to bring a year of happiness. Throughout Scandinavia, *æbleskiver*, distinctive puffy, spherical pancakes cooked in a special cast-iron pan with little hollows, are particularly associated with Christmas-morning breakfast. For the Jewish celebration of lights—Hannukah—grated potato pancakes, latkes, are enjoyed with huge relish.

Pancakes are probably one of our earliest foods, dating back to prehistoric times when plant grains were ground into flour, mixed with water, and cooked on a flat stone over burning embers. Grinding tools dating back more than 30,000 years have been found, which suggests pancakes were popular even among Stone Age humans. We probably have the Romans to thank for the invention of the pancake as known today. One of the first recipes for a sweet batter cooked over a griddle, dating back to the fourth century, is accredited to Apicus, the legendary Roman gourmet, and consists of egg, milk, and water, beaten with a little flour, fried, and served with pepper and honey. Many pancake recipes from around the globe use gluten-free flours: from quinoa to coconut, and are not exclusively grains—think chestnut and chickpea—and these are important to living and eating more cleanly and sustainably with regard to both our body and planet.

Strictly speaking, a pancake is starch-based and poured as a batter onto a hot surface to be cooked free form or in a mold. Although proverbially flat, when made with the right ingredients—baking powder, baking soda, yeast, beaten egg white, or carbonated water—they may rise and be supremely fluffy. The fluffiest in this book are German pancakes known as "Dutch babies" ("Dutch" in this instance meaning "Deutsch"), and Finnish *pannukakku*, both of which are baked in the oven. I've taken some latitude and included a number of closely related potato-based pancakes, too, from Persian *kuku* and Irish boxty to supremely light and delectable baked-potato pancakes.

PANCAKE-MAKING PROWESS

Although making pancakes of all sorts of persuasions is relatively quick and easy, there's plenty to consider in making near-perfect pancakes that are not too dense, nor unevenly cooked, nor flat when they're meant to be gloriously fluffy and, frankly, irresistible. Here are my tips on what to consider.

INGREDIENTS AND WEIGHING

Use good quality, unbleached preferably organic flour and consider ancient grains such as spelt and einkorn. For crêpes, bread flour really does give incredibly light results. Gluten-free flour and baking powder can be substituted throughout. Eggs should be free-range, organic, and large. They have bigger, more flavorful yolks that cook and taste better. I always use unsalted butter unless otherwise specified. Unrefined sugar is far better and I often substitute coconut sugar. Organic lemons make a difference too. Always measure ingredients to make sure the ratios are correct. Guesswork isn't good enough for pancakes.

HOW TO WHISK

For British pancakes and French crêpes, it is fine to whisk the batter with a hand mixer. For US-style pancakes, *dorayaki*, and where a fluffy pancake is imperative, be very wary of overmixing. Instead, whisk by hand until the wet ingredients are just incorporated into the dry ingredients and fold in egg whites with a metal spoon or spatula. Don't worry about banishing the batter of all its lumps.

RESTING

Where recipes recommend that you rest the batter, it really does make a difference, however impatient you're inclined to be. The pancakes will be distinctly more even in texture because the starch has had more time to absorb the liquid, and the air bubbles will have risen and dispersed.

USING THE CORRECT PAN

I manage extremely well with a good nonstick frying pan with a low lip to make for better flipping. With stainless steel pans, opt for either a shallow-lipped crêpe pan or omelet pan with sides curving bowl-like into the base. These are far longer lasting and should be seasoned before first use, as should sturdy and reliable cast-iron pans. To season, pour a thin layer of vegetable oil into the pan, add 2 tablespoons of table salt, heat until smoking (the salt will blacken), then turn off the heat. Armed with oven mitts and paper towels, scour the inside purposefully. Let cool and wipe out again with more paper towels. Ideally, these pans should not be washed, just wiped with paper towels. For a more thorough clean, use hot water and a sponge, but not dish soap, and then reseason. Their natural nonstick qualities should improve with age. The recipes for *æbelskiver*, *poffertjes*, and hoppers require special pans, but all are widely and inexpensively available online or at ethnic shops. You can always use electric griddles for cooking pancakes, especially if regularly cooking for large numbers. They give good, even results, although I think they take away some of the romance of making pancakes. Pancakes can be made on an Aga too.

HEATING AND GREASING THE PAN

Temperature is key. The pan should be shimmering hot, so that a few drops of water flipped on the surface bounce and skitter before evaporating. Be sure, however, that it is not so hot as to scorch the pancakes. Start medium–high and adjust. Whether using oil or butter, use sparingly. It is imperative that it heats evenly, otherwise the pancakes are likely to burn in some areas and undercook in others. I recommend using paper towels to smear the pan or, better still, a silicon or heatproof pastry brush, but be sure to wipe off any excess. Use either unsalted butter, which has a lower whey content and burns less easily, or a mixture of butter and oil, which is also less likely to burn. Ideally, clarify the butter first by melting it in a small pan. When bubbling, skim off the foamy milk proteins that rise to the surface and pour the clarified butter beneath into a small bowl.

MOVING THE PANCAKE AND FLIPPING

Don't be tempted to move the pancake too soon, although using a spatula to check the underside is acceptable. A good indicator is that the edges of the pancake are slightly dry and don't form crumbs on the palette knife. One of the very best checks is to wait for bubbles to not only form but also to burst in the center. Only flip once, as repeated flipping will cause pancakes to deflate or turn rubbery.

FLIPPING TECHNIQUE

The best way to flip is to hold the pan handle firmly with two hands and to jerk it upward and slightly forward with a sharp movement. As the pancake takes off, pull the pan back to catch it. It's a skill worth practicing to wow guests. Pancakes can, however, be flipped with a spatula too.

KEEPING PANCAKES WARM

Ideally, pancakes should be eaten immediately. The best way to keep flat pancakes or crêpes warm is to layer them between sheets of parchment paper and place in a low 225°F oven for 5 to 10 minutes maximum. For other pancakes, set them out in a single layer on a wire rack on baking sheet and keep them warm in a similarly low oven.

FREEZING PANCAKES

Pancakes can be frozen. Place a sheet of parchment paper between each pancake and stack them together. Wrap the pancakes tightly in foil or put them inside a heavy-duty freezer bag and freeze. Use frozen pancakes within 1 month for the best results. Defrost and reheat in the oven.

Breakfast & Brunch

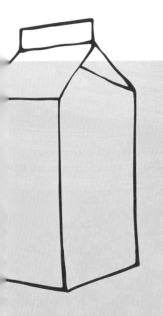

Scottish Oat Pancakes

WITH SKYR, RASPBERRIES, AND THYME HONEY

This is oatmeal in the form of a pancake, so it's comforting, like a warm bear hug. These pancakes, with their subtle, toasty taste, make a perfect start for breakfast or brunch, or as a dessert. Porridge oats are simply processed in a food processor to make a fine flour. Besides oatmeal, this oat pancake gets me thinking about Scottish cranachan, so I've paired it with skyr—the Icelandic yogurt that is similar to Greek yogurt with a rich, creamy texture—raspberries, and thyme honey. The oat pancakes would work equally well as a savory breakfast dish, especially as a "full Scottish" with bacon, blood sausage (haggis, if you dare!), roasted tomato, thyme-butter sautéed mushrooms, and a poached egg.

PREP 10 mins

COOK 10 mins

TOTAL 20 mins

DIETARY

*USE GLUTEN-FREE
SELF-RISING FLOUR*

MAKES

*12 TO 16 x 4IN,
SERVES 4*

1¾ cups porridge oats
1¼ cups self-rising flour
½ teaspoon ground cinnamon
2 large eggs, separated
1¾ cups milk, or soy or almond milk
3 tablespoons butter, melted

9-ounce container skyr or Greek yogurt
fresh raspberries
6 tablespoons thyme honey

Preheat the oven to 225°F and warm a plate to keep the pancakes warm while you make them. Process the porridge oats in a food processor to make a flour.

Mix the processed porridge oats, flour, and cinnamon together in a bowl. Whisk in the egg yolks and the milk. Put the egg whites in a clean bowl and whisk until they form soft peaks. Gently fold the whites into the batter. The batter will be fairly thick, like heavy cream.

Heat a heavy nonstick frying pan over high heat. Reduce to medium–high and use a heatproof pastry brush to brush with butter. Pour in a ladleful of batter and cook for 1 to 2 minutes until it puffs up. Flip over and cook for 2 minutes or until lightly golden. Keep the pancakes warm and repeat with the remaining batter, adding more butter to the pan as necessary. Serve the pancakes with a scoop of skyr or Greek yogurt, a scattering of raspberries, and a good drizzle of thyme honey.

Fluffy Ricotta Pancakes

WITH RASPBERRIES AND HONEYCOMB, LIME, AND GINGER BUTTER

Like sublime fluffy clouds, the texture of these pancakes is ridiculously light and delicate. Australian king of breakfast, Bill Granger, first introduced me to them even before he opened Granger & Co. in London. I was blown away. They're very different from most pancakes, as they get their exceptionally light texture from the combination of ricotta and whipped egg white. Really, they are more like soufflé hotcakes than pancakes in both looks and taste. They are ideal for breakfast (they're not too messy for breakfast in bed!), and they're superb as a dessert, too, with infinite accompaniments. I also like to serve them with tangy baked rhubarb, orange, and fresh ginger compote. For Aussie authenticity, I have simply borrowed Bill Granger's classic honeycomb butter with lime and fresh ginger.

PREP 20 mins
plus up to 1 hour chilling

COOK 20 mins

TOTAL 40 mins

DIETARY

USE GLUTEN-FREE FLOUR

MAKES

20 x 4IN, SERVES 4 TO 6

9-ounce container of ricotta, strained

2 large eggs, separated

¾ cup all-purpose flour, sifted

1 teaspoon baking powder

salt

zest of 2 limes

½ cup low-fat milk

4 tablespoons coconut oil

9 ounces raspberries, or 2 bananas, sliced

FOR THE HONEYCOMB BUTTER

10 tablespoons (1 stick + 2 tablespoons) unsalted butter, at room temperature

zest of 1 lime

1 tablespoon lime juice

1¼-inch piece of fresh ginger, peeled and finely grated

3 ounces fresh honeycomb

To make the honeycomb butter, cream the butter until soft, then add the lime zest and juice and the ginger. Gradually beat in the honeycomb. Shape into a long roll, then wrap in plastic wrap and put in the freezer for 15 minutes or in the fridge for 1 hour to firm up.

Put the ricotta and egg yolks in a large bowl and mix together. Add the flour, baking powder, and a pinch of salt, then add the lime zest and milk and whisk to make a smooth batter.

Beat the egg white until foamy using a whisk, then gently fold into the ricotta mixture making sure not to knock the lightness out of the egg. (The mixture will keep overnight in the fridge at this stage.)

Heat a frying pan or griddle over medium heat and add 1 tablespoon coconut oil. Drop in two large heaping spoonfuls of batter and flatten to a circle, then add batter for a few more pancakes. Cook for 1 to 2 minutes until they begin to bubble and turn lightly golden. Flip over and cook for 1 to 2 minutes until lightly golden, being careful to not let them burn.

Put the pancakes on a plate and cover with a tent of foil; this is preferable to putting them in the oven as they are so delicate that they would dry out. Repeat with the remaining batter, adding more coconut oil to the pan as before. Serve them warm with generous slices of the honeycomb butter and fresh raspberries (or sliced banana when raspberries are not in season).

Spiced Spelt Pancake Stack

WITH APPLE-POACHED BLACKBERRIES

The comforting flavor of the cinnamon, cardamom and nutmeg spice mix conjures up *hygge*, a very distinctive sense of coziness that the Danes like to cultivate. Spelt flour gives an addictiveness nuttiness to the pancakes, and buttermilk adds a little sourness. Try sprouted spelt flour, too, for extra flavor and goodness. The pancakes won't firm up as much as non-buttermilk pancakes, so make sure they are sufficiently set before flipping them. They are perfectly good with maple syrup alone, although they go extraordinarily well with this fragrant blackberry and apple sauce. Bacon would make a good accompaniment for breakfast too.

PREP   10 mins

* plus 30 mins resting

COOK   35 mins

TOTAL   45 mins

DIETARY

SPELT FLOUR IS
GLUTEN-FREE

MAKES

8 x 4IN,
SERVES 4

2 cups spelt flour, sifted
1½ teaspoons baking powder
pinch of salt
2 tablespoons superfine sugar
2 teaspoons freshly grated nutmeg
1 teaspoon cardamom seeds, crushed
2 teaspoons ground cinnamon
3 tablespoons butter, melted
1¾ cups buttermilk, plus extra
1 large egg
melted butter, for cooking

FOR THE POACHED BLACKBERRIES
2 cups apple juice
strips of zest from 1 orange
1 cinnamon stick
3 star anise
3 cloves
2 tablespoons wildflower honey
2 cups blackberries
1¼ cups crème fraîche

Put the flour in a bowl, add the baking powder, salt, and sugar, then stir in the spices and then the butter. Whisk the buttermilk and egg together, then slowly add to the batter mixture using a metal spoon. (Don't be surprised if the batter remains a little lumpy. It should take 2 to 3 seconds to drop from the spoon. If it is too thick, add more buttermilk; too liquid, add more flour.) Cover and rest in the fridge for at least 30 minutes, or make it the night before.

Preheat the oven to 225°F and put a baking sheet with a wire rack inside in the oven for keeping the pancakes warm while you make them. Meanwhile, to make the poached blackberries, put the apple juice in a pan over medium–low heat and add the orange zest, cinnamon stick, star anise, and cloves. Gently heat to infuse, then add the honey. Add the blackberries and gently warm through, but don't overcook, as the fruit should remain whole. Remove from the heat.

Heat a large nonstick frying pan over medium heat and use a heatproof pastry brush to brush with butter. When the butter starts to foam, add 2 ladlefuls of batter to make a pancake, tip the pan to ensure the batter is evenly distributed in the pan, then cook for 1½ minutes or until almost set, bubbles start to form and pop on the surface, and the underneath is golden. Flip over and cook for 1½ minutes or until lightly golden. Transfer to the wire rack in the oven. Repeat with the remaining batter, adding more butter to the pan as necessary. Serve with the poached blackberries and a dollop of crème fraîche.

Scotch Pancakes

WITH CHERRY TOMATOES, MUSHROOMS, AND SAUSAGE

I remember being obsessed with Scotch pancakes from a package when I was young and often having them with jam as a treat when I came in from school. Nowadays I prefer them savory with a little Parmesan, as a nod to the many Italians who settled in Scotland in the nineteenth century. For an excellent breakfast to set oneself up for a long hike or as a reward at the end of a good morning's walk, combine with roasted tomatoes, grilled mushrooms, and breakfast sausage. For an even more substantial breakfast, add some scrambled eggs with chives. For a sweet version, omit the Parmesan and herbs, and add 2 tablespoons of superfine sugar and a dash of vanilla extract. Serve simply with jam or fruit.

PREP 10 mins

COOK 20 mins

TOTAL 30 mins

DIETARY

USE GLUTEN-FREE
FLOUR

MAKES

12 x 4IN,
SERVES 4

FOR THE TOMATOES

2 cups cherry tomatoes

2 tablespoons extra virgin olive oil

1 teaspoon chopped oregano leaves

14 ounces mushrooms, cleaned and
stalks trimmed

7 ounces breakfast sausage, sliced

mustard, to serve

FOR THE PANCAKES

1 cup self-rising flour

2 to 3 tablespoons grated Parmesan

salt and freshly ground black pepper

1 tablespoon chopped oregano leaves

1 large egg, beaten

⅔ cup low-fat milk

3 tablespoons sunflower or canola oil

Preheat the oven to 350°F. Put the tomatoes for the broiler in a roasting pan, drizzle with 1 tablespoon of the oil, and scatter with the oregano. Roast for 15 minutes, then reduce to 225°F and put a plate in the oven to keep the pancakes warm as you make them.

Meanwhile, for the pancakes, sift the flour into a large bowl. Mix in the Parmesan, a pinch of salt, and the oregano. Add the egg and the milk, and incorporate with an immersion blender. The batter will be thick and creamy. There is no need to let this stand.

Heat a large, heavy frying pan over medium heat and add 1 tablespoon sunflower oil. Spread evenly with paper towels. Pour in 3 large spoonfuls of the batter and use the tip of the spoon to form an even circle about 4 inches in diameter. Add the batter for one or two more pancakes if it will fit. Cook for 2 minutes until almost set, bubbles start to form and pop on the surface, and the underneath is golden. Flip over with a spatula and cook for 1 to 2 minutes until golden. Stack on the warmed plate while cooking the rest of the pancakes, or better yet keep warm in the oven on a baking sheet. Use a little more oil for each batch.

Preheat the broiler or a griddle pan. Season the mushrooms with salt and pepper, then drizzle with the remaining olive oil. Place stalk-side up on the grill rack or pan. Cook for 1 to 2 minutes, then turn over and cook for 3 to 4 minutes until golden. Don't move the mushrooms around too much while cooking, as this releases the natural juices and makes them soggy.

At the same time, broil or pan-fry the sausage for 2 to 3 minutes on each side until lovely and crisp. Serve the Scotch pancakes with the tomatoes, mushrooms, and sausage along with a good dollop of mustard.

Irish Boxty

Boxty is a traditional Irish potato pancake made with a mixture of cooked, mashed, and grated raw potato. Its texture is part pancake, part hash brown. In Gaelic, boxty translates as "poor man's bread," as it was often served for breakfast in place of bread as an economical alternative. I can't help being amused by an old rhyme, "Boxty on the griddle, boxty in the pan, if you can't make boxty, you'll never get a man." My version is made with egg white and buttermilk for extra fluffiness, and with whole grain mustard and chopped parsley for full on flavor has plenty of power! I like to serve boxty with poached smoked haddock, spinach, poached eggs, and a mustardy crème fraîche sauce to finish, for an Irish-inspired breakfast or brunch.

PREP 20 mins

COOK 30 mins

TOTAL 50 mins

DIETARY

USE GLUTEN-FREE FLOUR; AND USE RICE FLOUR MILK IN PLACE OF BUTTERMILK

MAKES

16 x 3in, SERVES 4

10½ ounces Russet potatoes, coarsely grated

10½ ounces potatoes, peeled, cooked, and mashed

2¾ cups all-purpose flour, sifted

1 teaspoon baking powder

sea salt and freshly ground black pepper

2 tablespoons unsalted butter, melted, plus extra for cooking

1 large egg white

¾ cup buttermilk

2 tablespoons whole grain mustard

¼ cup chopped parsley leaves

1 tablespoons sunflower or canola oil

FOR THE HADDOCK AND EGGS

¾ cup low-fat milk

4 fillets of smoked haddock

2 tablespoons butter, cut into cubes

a splash of white wine vinegar

4 large eggs

1¼ pounds baby spinach

FOR THE SAUCE

¾ cup crème fraîche

4 teaspoons whole grain mustard

juice of ½ lemon

a handful of parsley leaves, chopped

Preheat the oven to 225°F and put a baking sheet in the oven to keep the pancakes warm while you make them. Put the grated potato in a fine-mesh strainer set over medium bowl and add a little salt. Toss well to mix, then press the grated potatoes against the sides of the strainer to remove any liquid.

Add the grated potatoes to the mashed potatoes. Add the flour and baking powder, then mix gently. Season with plenty of pepper, then stir in the melted butter.

Lightly whisk the egg white in a medium bowl. Add the buttermilk and whisk again to combine. Fold into the potato and flour mixture until evenly incorporated. Add the mustard and parsley, and stir in gently.

Heat a large nonstick frying pan or grill pan over medium heat. The pan is hot enough when water sprinkled onto the surface bounces and splutters; it is too hot if it evaporates instantly. Once the pan is ready, add 1 tablespoon oil and a pat of butter, and melt it gently. Drop four dollops of batter from a little height to spread into freeform boxty in the pan about ½-inch thick. Cook for 4 minutes or until the pancakes are golden and crisp on the outside. Flip over and cook on the other side until golden.

Transfer to the baking sheet in the oven. Repeat with the remaining batter, adding more oil and butter to the pan as necessary.

Meanwhile, to prepare the haddock, pour the milk into a wide-based saucepan or frying pan and season with a little salt. Bring to a simmer and add the haddock, skin-side down. Put the cubes of butter on top and cook for 6 to 8 minutes until it is opaque and flakes easily. Remove from the milk to serve.

While the fish is poaching, bring a small frying pan of water to a boil, add a splash of vinegar, and carefully add the eggs, leaving space between them. Cook for 2 to 5 minutes or until the white is set and the yolk is creamy or to your liking.

Meanwhile, put the spinach leaves in a colander over the sink. Carefully pour over boiling water to wilt, then squeeze out as much water as possible using your hands or a wooden spoon. Set aside.

To make the sauce, put the crème fraîche in a small pan over medium heat and add the mustard. Heat through, stirring, until it is smooth, then add the lemon juice and parsley.

Serve the boxty with the smoked haddock placed on top of the spinach and a poached egg on the side with a liberal helping of mustard and crème fraîche sauce.

Fluffiest-Ever Pancakes

WITH BACON, MAPLE SYRUP, AND AVOCADO

For many Scots and Brits, obsession with pancakes began with discovering the greedy pleasures of American pancakes. The quintessential American-style pancake is ethereally light and fluffy, yet crisp on the outside and served in a "devour-me" stack topped with bacon and an indecent amount of maple syrup cascading down its sides. What gives these pancakes such a brilliant texture is using a little baking powder and baking soda, plus buttermilk. The baking soda reacts with the acid in the batter mix to produce bubbles of carbon dioxide, which makes for a lighter-than-air finish. The most heavenly plump yet gossamer-light pancakes I've ever eaten were from the Clinton Street Bakery in New York where they serve pancakes breakfast, noon, and night, getting through more than 2,000 eggs in a week. Almost every order I saw emerge included pancakes. I follow owner Neil Kleinberg's advice to be extremely careful about how delicately I incorporate the egg whites into the batter, and that makes all the difference to their supreme fluffiness. At Clinton Street Bakery, the most popular pancake order is with blueberries. Never add blueberries to the batter; just scatter them on the top of the pancake as it cooks, and push them into the batter, otherwise the blueberries will bleed. At Clinton Street Bakery, pancakes are invariably served with the bakery's own maple salted-butter sauce, which is incredibly easy to replicate at home.

PREP 15 mins

COOK 15 mins

TOTAL 30 mins

DIETARY

USE GLUTEN-FREE ALL-PURPOSE FLOUR

MAKES

*8 x 5IN,
SERVES 4*

2 cups all-purpose flour, sifted
2 teaspoons baking powder
1 teaspoon baking soda
1 teaspoon salt
3 teaspoons superfine sugar
2 cups buttermilk
4 tablespoons butter, melted, plus
3 tablespoons
2 large eggs, separated
1 cup blueberries (optional)

FOR THE MAPLE SALTED-BUTTER
SAUCE
½ cup maple syrup
8 tablespoons (1 stick) cold, unsalted
butter, cubed

TO SERVE
8 slices thick-cut bacon
2 avocados, halved, pitted, and peeled
zest and juice of 1 lime
sea salt and freshly ground pepper
maple syrup, for drizzling

Preheat the oven to 250°F and put a baking sheet with a wire rack inside in the oven for keeping the pancakes warm. In a large bowl, whisk together the flour, baking powder, baking soda, salt, and sugar. In a separate bowl gently whisk the buttermilk with the 4 tablespoons butter and the egg yolks. Put the egg whites in a clean, grease-free bowl and whisk until they form medium peaks yet are still soft in the middle—do not overwhisk. Gently fold half the egg whites into the batter using the whisk at first and then a spatula, turning the bowl while folding. Add the remaining egg whites in the same way. The batter should be slightly lumpy for the best results, with large parts of egg white not fully incorporated.

Heat a nonstick crêpe pan over medium heat until hot. The pan is hot enough when water sprinkled onto the surface bounces and splutters; it is too hot if it evaporates instantly. Turn the heat down to medium–low. Brush the pan with 1 tablespoon melted butter and wipe off any excess with paper towels. (Using butter ensures an extra-crisp finish.)

Drop 2 to 3 tablespoons of the batter into the pan from the tip of the tablespoon for each pancake. This is the time to scatter with the blueberries, if using. Cook for 2 minutes or until bubbles start to form and pop on the surface of the pancake and it is slightly dry and airy around the edges and lightly golden underneath. Flip over and cook for 2 minutes or until lightly golden. Keep the pancakes warm on the rack in the oven. Repeat with the remaining batter, adding more butter to the pan as necessary.

Meanwhile, fry the bacon in a dry frying pan over high heat, or under a preheated broiler, for 5 minutes. Mash up the avocados with a fork, then mix in the lime zest and juice, and season with black pepper.

To make the maple salted-butter sauce, if using, heat the maple syrup in a small saucepan over medium heat. Whisk in the cold butter until it is incorporated and the sauce is smooth. Remove from the heat and keep warm until ready to use.

Serve a stack of pancakes, topped with the smashed avocado, crisp bacon, and an indecent amount of maple syrup drizzled over, or serve with the maple salted-butter sauce.

Poffertjes

The name *poffertjes* refers to the way the pancakes puff up as they're turned in their special *poffertjes* pan, which has lots of little dimple-like indentations. *Poffertjes* are an integral part of every Dutch celebration, and are a particular feature of Christmas markets with street vendors cooking them in huge batches. Written recipes first appeared in the mid 1700s, when they were made with only buckwheat flour, yeast, and water, and were considered a poor man's meal. Eggs, milk, and a little sugar were later additions. I prefer lighter *poffertjes* made with 50:50 wheat and buckwheat. Their light, spongy texture, crisp finish, and slightly fermented taste is irresistible. A huge platter of hot *poffertjes*, served traditionally doused in confectioners' sugar with melted butter, is a superb treat after a long wintery shopping spree or a walk in the park. Although the Dutch never eat them for breakfast, *poffertjes* make a heavenly indulgent sweet brunch dish, especially served with cranberry and orange compete and coconut yogurt.

PREP 10 mins

* plus 1 hour resting

COOK 10 mins

TOTAL 20 mins

DIETARY

USE GLUTEN-FREE FLOURS

MAKES

ABOUT 40 x 1 IN, SERVES 6

1 teaspoon fast-acting yeast
1 cup warm milk
¾ cup buckwheat flour
¾ cup all-purpose flour
pinch of salt
1 teaspoon superfine sugar
2 large eggs
2 tablespoons butter, melted

2½ tablespoons confectioners' sugar

FOR THE COMPOTE
2 tablespoons brown sugar
3 organic oranges, blood oranges if available, peeled and sliced
2½ cups cranberries, fresh or frozen
1¼ cups coconut yogurt, optional

Preheat the oven to 225°F and warm a plate.

Mix the yeast with 3 tablespoons of the warm milk and stir until dissolved. Sift the flours and salt into a large bowl and add the sugar, yeast mixture, and eggs. Combine well, then gradually add the remaining milk, whisking well between each addition until the batter is smooth and the consistency of heavy cream. Set aside to rest, covered with plastic wrap, for at least 1 hour.

After resting, stir the batter again. Ideally, use a funnel to fill a small squeezy bottle with the batter, which will make it easier to fill the shallow hollows of the pan. Believe me, this is very pleasing and makes things far less messy.

Heat the *poffertjes* pan over medium–high heat, then quickly brush each indentation with melted butter. When the butter is sizzling, squirt in enough batter to fill each indentation or use a tablespoon or ladle dexterously. Cook for 1 minute, until bubbles start to form and pop on the surface and they become crisp at the edges. Deftly and rapidly turn the *poffertjes* using two forks. The underneath should be puffy and lightly golden. Cook for 1 minute. To serve traditionally, simply pile *poffertjes* onto a warm plate, dredge with confectioners' sugar, and anoint with melted butter. For a winter treat, add cranberry and orange compote and coconut yogurt.

For the compote, put the sugar and 2 tablespoons of water in a pan and heat to dissolve the sugar. Once bubbling, add the orange and cranberries. Stir, then turn up the heat and leave to bubble for a few minutes until most of the liquid has evaporated and the compote is thick and sticky.

Potato Latkes

FRIED EGG, SUMAC, AVOCADO, AND TAHINI HUMMUS

Potato pancakes are very much in vogue currently and it is difficult to resist their crisp, brown, wonderfully crunchy temptation. For me they are synonymous with my childhood. My great-grandmother would make incredible latkes to celebrate Hanukkah, the Jewish festival of lights commemorating Judah Maccabee recapturing the Holy Temple in Jerusalem in 164BCE after it had been desecrated by the Syrian King Antiochus III. Miraculously, the flame for the eternal lamp continued to burn for eight days even though there scarcely seemed enough oil for one day. Hence, the treat of latkes fried in copious oil.

In my family, there's much dispute as to whether the potatoes should be grated or shredded in a food processor. Call me old-fashioned, but I still prefer to grate them. There's also heated discussion as to whether the potatoes should have their starch rinsed out, or collected in a strainer and returned to the pan. I tend to dispense with the starch. Latkes make a good sidekick to roast chicken or baked salmon, too, although for a snack or appetizer it is hard to beat the traditional (and, for me, nostalgic) accompaniments of cinnamon-scented applesauce and sour cream. If you find yourself in New York, don't miss the latkes at Russ & Daughters served with smoked salmon and sour cream. For a rather different twist, Alsatian potato pancake recipes are made like latkes adding nutmeg and parsley to the mix. I also like Polish ratzelech: potato pancakes served with herring, beets, and horseradish.

PREP 30 mins

COOK 20 mins

TOTAL 50 mins

DIETARY

USE GLUTEN-FREE FLOUR

MAKES

12 x 4IN, SERVES 4

FOR THE AVOCADO HUMMUS

1 avocado, halved, pitted, and peeled

zest and juice of ½ lemon

1 x 14-ounce can chickpeas, drained and rinsed

2 tablespoons tahini

1 garlic clove, crushed

3 tablespoons finely chopped cilantro leaves

3 tablespoons olive oil, plus extra if needed

FOR THE LATKES

4 large potatoes

1 onion

3 tablespoons chopped parsley leaves

1 large egg, lightly beaten

2 tablespoons all-purpose flour

½ teaspoon baking powder

salt and freshly ground pepper

sunflower oil or canola oil, for cooking

FOR THE FRIED EGGS

4 tablespoons olive oil

4 large eggs

juice of 1 lemon

a sprinkle of sumac

To make the avocado and tahini hummus, blend all the ingredients in a food processor until they are incorporated into a thick, slightly whippy texture. Depending on the ripeness of the avocado, it might be necessary to add a little more olive oil or water.

For the latkes, coarsely grate the potatoes and onion, alternating between onion and potato, as the acid in the onion helps to prevent the potato from discoloring. Transfer the potato mixture to a colander and squeeze the mixture by hand to remove as much liquid as possible (this is really important, as the latkes won't crisp up if they are too watery). Transfer the mixture to a large bowl and stir in the parsley, egg, flour, and baking powder, then season with salt and pepper.

Heat 2 tablespoons oil in a large nonstick pan over medium heat until it is shimmering. Spoon 2 tablespoons of the potato mixture into the pan for each latke. Flatten with the back of a spoon so that each is about 3 to 4 inches in diameter. Cook for 4 minutes or until golden underneath and crisp. Turn the latkes carefully using 2 spatulas so that the oil doesn't splatter, and cook for 4 minutes until golden and crisp. It is a good idea to stir the potato mixture between cooking the batches.

While the latkes are cooking, make the fried eggs with sumac. Heat a heavy frying pan over medium–high heat and add 2 tablespoons of the oil. Cook 2 eggs at a time. Crack the eggs into the pan, wait until the whites are setting a little, and then squeeze a little lemon juice over each, being careful, as it may splatter. Cook until set. Sprinkle with sumac before serving.

Shakshuka Quinoa & Buckwheat Pancakes

WITH EGGS AND HARISSA YOGURT

Strictly speaking, shakshuka is a tomato- and pepper-rich vegetable stew baked with egg. Enjoyed throughout the Middle East and Tunisia, it has become an insanely popular brunch dish with its potent mix of spicy flavors, thanks largely to chef Yotam Ottolenghi. I've taken liberties and used a shakshuka-inspired sauce with smoked paprika inside quinoa flour and buckwheat crêpes with harissa-spiked yogurt and a poached egg to make a more substantial, all-around brunch dish. The crepe-like pancakes have a distinctive earthiness to them, which contrasts well with the shakshuka.

PREP 20 mins

* plus 30 mins resting

COOK 30 mins

TOTAL 50 mins

DIETARY

QUINOA AND
BUCKWHEAT FLOUR
ARE GLUTEN-FREE

MAKES

8 x 10IN,
SERVES 4

1 cup quinoa flour
½ cup buckwheat flour
pinch of salt
2 large eggs, beaten
1¼ cups low-fat milk
1 tablespoon unsalted butter, melted
sunflower oil or canola oil, for cooking
a splash of vinegar
4 eggs
salt and freshly ground pepper

FOR THE SHAKSHUKA
1 teaspoon cumin seeds
2 tablespoons extra virgin olive oil
1 onion, thinly sliced
1 red and 1 green bell pepper, seeded and diced
2 garlic cloves, crushed

2 teaspoons smoked paprika
a large pinch of saffron threads
pinch of cayenne pepper, or to taste
1 x 14-ounce can tomatoes, or ripe fresh tomatoes
2 teaspoons sugar
a large bunch of cilantro, leaves finely chopped
salt and freshly ground black pepper

FOR THE HARISSA YOGURT
2 teaspoons harissa paste
1 tablespoon lemon juice
1 garlic clove, crushed
1 tablespoon olive oil
a large bunch of parsley, finely chopped
1 cup Greek yogurt

Preheat the oven to 225°F and heat a plate to keep the pancakes warm while you make them.

Sift the flours and salt into a bowl. Make a well in the center. Whisk in the eggs one at a time using a whisk or hand mixer to create a thick, smooth batter. Gradually whisk in the milk, followed by the melted butter. Set aside to rest for 30 minutes.

Meanwhile, to make the shakshuka, dry roast the cumin seeds in a large saucepan over medium heat, tossing regularly until they begin to pop. Add the olive oil and onion and cook for 5 minutes or until golden. Add the bell peppers and cook until soft. Stir in the garlic and the remaining spices and herbs. Cook for another 3 minutes.

Add the tomatoes and sugar, then mash them down with a wooden spoon and bring them to a boil. Reduce the heat and simmer for 20 minutes or until the consistency of a thick pasta sauce. Season with salt and pepper. Add more cayenne for a spicier finish, if you like, and stir in the cilantro.

To make the harissa yogurt, put the harissa paste in a small bowl and add the lemon juice, garlic, oil, parsley, and yogurt. Whisk together, then set aside.

While the shakshuka is cooking, make the pancakes: Put a large frying pan over medium heat. Use paper towels to wipe the pan with a good coating of sunflower oil. Pour a small ladleful of batter into the middle of the pan, tilting it quickly so that the batter covers the base thinly. Reduce the heat a little and cook for 1 to 2 minutes until almost set, bubbles start to form and pop on the surface, and the underneath is pale golden. Flip over with a spatula and cook until pale golden—the second side will cook slightly more quickly. Turn out of the pan. Repeat with the remaining batter, adding more oil to the pan as necessary. Stack the pancakes on the warmed plate, interleaved with wax paper.

Meanwhile, make the poached eggs: Bring a small frying pan of water to a boil, add a splash of vinegar, and carefully add the eggs, leaving space between them. Cook for 2 to 5 minutes or until the white is set and the yolk is creamy or to your liking. Lift from the pan using a slotted spoon to serve.

Lay the pancakes out on a flat surface. Put 2 spoonfuls of shakshuka sauce in the middle of each crêpe, tuck the sides in, and roll up. Serve with the harissa yogurt spooned over and the poached eggs alongside.

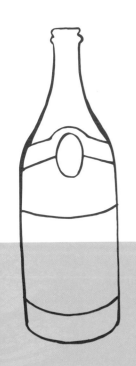

Snacks
& Nibbles

Socca

Socca, made with chickpea flour, olive oil, and water, is so simple, and so redolent of sunny Nice and the French Riviera. I especially like it with homemade anchoïade and crème fraîche, although pistou or tapenade are great accompaniments too. I first tried it in Nice's Cours Saleya market—the socca is transported there from a bakery deep in the Old Town on the back of a bicycle, and it smells so enticing. Chez Pipo on the edge of Nice Old Town, however, is the real deal. Here the socca is cooked over a mightily impressive wood fire and has a satisfyingly deep, earthy, smoky tang. I am impressed, however, by just how good socca made in a frying pan tastes, especially with the addition of a generous teaspoon of cumin, which adds toasty notes that hint at a wood fire. Folding in two egg whites makes for a lighter socca, although it is not essential and definitely not how the Niçoise make it. In Nice market, socca is served cut into triangles and sprinkled with sea salt. I find it makes a rather good appetizer or party snack. It is extra-good with a special seaweed salt, or even a truffle salt.

PREP   15 mins
* plus 30 mins resting

COOK   20 mins

TOTAL   35 mins

DIETARY

CHICKPEA FLOUR IS
GLUTEN-FREE

MAKES

12 TO 16 X 4IN,
OR 4 LARGE,
SERVES 4

1½ tablespoons olive oil, plus extra
for greasing
2¾ cups chickpea flour
½ teaspoon salt
a good grinding of black pepper
½ teaspoon ground cumin
2 cups tepid water
2 large egg whites

FOR THE ANCHOÏADE
3½-ounce jar of anchovies, drained
1 garlic clove, crushed
a good handful of flat-leaf
parsley leaves
3 to 4 tablespoons olive oil

To make the anchoïde, put the anchovies, garlic, and parsley in a food processor and pulse-blend, adding the olive oil gradually until it becomes a rough, thick paste. Set aside.

Preheat the oven to 225°F and line two baking sheets with parchment paper, then brush them lightly with olive oil. Put the chickpea flour in a large bowl and mix in the salt, pepper, and cumin. Gradually pour in the water, whisking with an electric hand mixer as you go. Continue whisking until the mixture is smooth and the consistency of heavy cream. Put the egg whites into a clean bowl and whisk until just stiff. Gently incorporate the egg whites into the socca mixture using a metal spoon. Don't be tempted to use a whisk. Let rest in the fridge for at least 30 minutes, or even prepare it first thing in the morning so it is ready for the evening.

Place a nonstick frying pan over high heat for 2 minutes, then reduce the heat to medium–high. Using a heatproof pastry brush, brush the pan with olive oil. Pour a ladleful of batter into the pan; the socca should be about ¼-inch thick. Cook for 2 minutes or until tiny bubbles start to form on the surface. Flip over and cook for 2 minutes or until lightly golden, a little crisp, and lacy. Transfer to the warmed baking sheets while you repeat with the remaining batter, adding more oil to the pan as necessary. Serve with bowls of anchoïade and crème fraîche for diners to dollop onto their socca. Accompany with a crisp salad and a well-chilled glass of rosé for instant transportation to Nice.

Farinata

WITH ROSEMARY AND SEA SALT OR PESTO

Traditionally, *farinata*, a baked chickpea pancake, is made in a wood-fired oven, although it works well started on the stove and finished in the oven. I adore it as an appetizer or as a simple dinner with a robust green salad and some charcuterie and cheese, especially crumbled Gorgonzola. Usually, it is just sprinkled with red onion, rosemary, and sea salt, and it's fantastic with a crisp wine or cold Italian beer. As the dish originates in Genoa, where the fishermen often eat it for breakfast in the early hours before setting out to sea, I also like to stir in some homemade pesto, which makes for an even more striking-looking and tasting *farinata*. Buy the best-quality chickpea flour you can source, preferably an Italian brand, for the tastiest of *farinata*. It will be called *farina di ceci*. Chickpea flour is now often found in the Indian sections of supermarkets (under gram flour) and good delis.

PREP   10 mins

* plus 4 hours or overnight resting

COOK   20 mins

TOTAL   30 mins

DIETARY

CHICKPEA FLOUR IS GLUTEN-FREE

MAKES

2 x 10IN SERVES 4 TO 6

4¼ cups sparkling water

2 teaspoons salt

3¼ cups chickpea flour, sifted

½ cup extra virgin olive oil

1 red onion, quartered and sliced into ultra-thin slivers

leaves from 2 large sprigs of rosemary

sea salt, to sprinkle

FOR THE BASIL PESTO

⅓ cup pine nuts

½ cup Parmesan, finely grated

1 garlic clove, crushed

3 ounces basil leaves

salt and freshly ground pepper

½ cup good-quality extra virgin olive oil

Pour the sparkling water into a bowl and add the salt and chickpea flour with 1½ tablespoons of the olive oil. Stir with a whisk to form a thick batter. Leave the mixture to stand at room temperature in a warmish place for 4 to 5 hours or, better still, overnight, so that the mixture can start fermenting, which gives the pancake a light, airy texture.

Preheat the oven to 400°F.

To make the pesto, if using this alternative, heat a small pan over medium–high heat and add the pine nuts. Cook to brown evenly, shaking the pan from time to time. Remove the pine nuts, retaining a few for garnish, and put the rest into a blender or food processor with the Parmesan, garlic, basil leaves, and seasoning. Process briefly. With the motor still running, gradually add the oil to make a smooth pesto. Set aside.

Heat a large, heavy ovenproof frying pan over medium–high heat until it's almost smoking. Using a heatproof pastry brush, brush the base generously with olive oil. Pour in the batter until no more than ¼-inch thick, and swirl it around so that the batter spreads out evenly. Cook for 1 to 2 minutes—the mixture will begin to bubble. Scatter with the onion slices and rosemary, or stir in 4 to 5 tablespoons of pesto and top with a scattering of pine nuts. Transfer the farinata to the oven for 10 to 12 minutes until set and the edges are crispy. Repeat with the remaining mixture. Serve sprinkled with sea salt and cut into wedges.

Blinis

WITH SMOKED SALMON, HORSERADISH, AND SOUR CREAM

Homemade blinis are a world apart from what the supermarkets offer up. They are warm, soft, doughy, fragrant, yeasty, and light. Authentic Russian blinis are made with buckwheat, which is not wheat at all, but a member of the rhubarb family, and has a slightly sour, nutty edge. I find it rather heavy used by itself, so tend to use a quarter buckwheat to three-quarters all-purpose flour. In Russia and other Eastern European countries, blinis are served at the beginning of Russian Orthodox Lent. The tradition dates back to pagan times when Maslenitsa, or the sun festival, was celebrated to mark the coming of spring. Round and golden blinis were thought to symbolize the sun and bring warmth.

PREP 15 mins

plus 30 mins resting

COOK 15 mins

TOTAL 30 mins

DIETARY

USE GLUTEN-FREE FLOUR

MAKES

20 x 3IN, SERVES 4 TO 6

3 tablespoons butter
¾ cup low-fat milk
1⅓ cups all-purpose flour (or use ⅓ cup buckwheat flour and 1 cup all-purpose flour, if you like), sifted
2 packages fast-acting yeast
pinch of superfine sugar
2 large eggs, separated
butter, for cooking

TO SERVE

1⅓ cups sour cream, smetana (Russian cultured cream), or crème fraiche
3 tablespoons creamed or grated fresh horseradish
7 ounces smoked salmon
a small bunch of dill
caviar (optional) (true Beluga or salmon roe, depending on budget)

Preheat the oven to 225°F and put in a rack on a baking sheet to keep the blinis warm.

Melt the butter in a small pan over medium heat, stir in the milk, and set aside. In a large bowl, mix together the flour, yeast, and sugar. Pour in the milk mixture. Beat the egg yolks lightly, then mix them gently into the batter. It will feel quite elastic. Set aside for 30 minutes at room temperature to ferment a little. Put the egg whites into a clean bowl and whisk until stiff and fluffy. Carefully and gently fold them into the batter.

Warm a nonstick frying pan or blini pan over medium heat and use paper towels to smear on a little butter. Put 2 heaping tablespoons of batter into the pan, then use the tip of the spoon to spread it into a circle. I make each about 3 inches in diameter. Add more batter to make 2 to 3 more pancakes in the pan at the same time. Leave them to spread, rise, and cook for up to 1 minute or until pale golden underneath. Flip over and cook for 40 seconds or until lightly golden. Keep warm in the oven and repeat with the remaining batter, adding more butter to the pan as necessary. (They can be wrapped up in packages of foil to reheat, too.)

Mix the sour cream with the horseradish in a small bowl. Serve the blinis in a generous pile with the smoked salmon and horseradish sour cream separately for constructing DIY blinis. Alternatively, spoon a little horseradish sour cream on top of each blini and top with strips of smoked salmon and sprigs of dill. If you're feeling fancy, bring out the caviar too!

Potato Blinis

A dreamy, wispy-light alternative to proper fermented blinis or more substantial potato pancakes, my potato blini recipe was first created by a chef–consultant friend, Philip Owens. Using fluffy baking potatoes is essential and they need to be baked for a good hour before making the blinis to ensure that they have the mesmerizing lightness. Philip always serves these with smoked eel, crispy bacon, and horseradish cream at Christmas, but I've adapted the recipe here for a summer party, topped with a delicately spiced crab cocktail.

PREP *10 mins*

★ plus 30 mins resting

COOK *75 mins*

TOTAL *85 mins*

10½ ounces Russet potatoes
2 large eggs, beaten, plus 2 egg whites
¼ cup heavy cream
¼ cup low-fat milk
1½ tablespoons all-purpose flour
butter, for cooking
¾ cup crème fraîche, to serve

FOR THE CRAB COCKTAIL TOPPING
1 dressed crab, or 7 ounces crabmeat
zest of 1 lime and 3 tablespoons lime juice
½ red chile, seeded and finely chopped
1 tablespoon finely chopped chives
1 tablespoon finely chopped flat-leaf parsley
1 tablespoon extra virgin olive oil
sea salt and freshly ground black

DIETARY

USE GLUTEN-FREE ALL-PURPOSE FLOUR

MAKES

20 X 2IN, SERVES 4 TO 6

Preheat the oven to 400°F. Bake the potatoes for 1 hour or until the insides are soft. Remove from the oven. Turn the oven down to 225°F and put a rack on a baking sheet inside to keep the blinis warm.

Meanwhile, put the crabmeat in a bowl and mix in the lime zest and juice, chile, herbs, and olive oil. Season with salt and pepper. Keep in the fridge until ready to use.

Push the cooked potato through a potato ricer or strainer into a bowl or food processor. Mix with the 2 beaten eggs, cream, milk, flour, and ½ teaspoon salt, either in the food processor or using a hand mixer. Pour into a large mixing bowl. Put the egg whites in a clean, grease-free bowl and whisk until they form soft peaks. Gently fold into the potato mixture using a spatula. Set aside to rest in a cool place for 30 minutes.

Place a large nonstick frying pan over medium–high heat. Add 1 teaspoon butter and swirl to coat the pan. Drop in tablespoonfuls of batter from the tip of a tablespoon, as many as will fit at one time. It will sizzle as it hits the pan. Cook for 2 minutes or until lightly golden. Flip over and cook for another 2 minutes, then keep warm in the oven. Repeat with the remaining batter, adding a little more butter to the pan as necessary.

The potato pancakes can also be made in advance and reheated in a preheated oven at 225°F on a baking sheet lined with parchment paper. If doing this, allow the pancakes to cool a little before topping them with crème fraîche; otherwise, it will melt and run off. Top with a dollop of crème fraîche and the crab cocktail before serving.

Cong You Bing
SCALLION PANCAKE

Rich, crisp, and addictive, these scallion pancakes are one of Northern China's most famous street foods, often found at breakfast "shops" or on dim sum menus. They are made with a dough of flour and hot water, rather than a batter, and shaped into snail-like coils and rolled to give them their distinctive flaky texture. Serve with a dipping sauce made with soy sauce, rice wine vinegar, and lime as a party snack or for a light supper.

PREP 30 mins

plus 30 mins resting

COOK 30 mins

TOTAL 60 mins

DIETARY

USE GLUTEN-FREE FLOUR

MAKES

16 x 3IN,
SERVES 8 AS A SNACK,
2 AS A MAIN MEAL

½ teaspoon sea salt

2¼ cups all-purpose flour, sifted, plus extra for dusting

sunflower oil

2 tablespoons toasted sesame oil

1 bunch of scallions, green parts and a little of the white finely chopped

1 tablespoon Chinese five-spice powder (optional)

FOR THE DIPPING SAUCE

¼ cup rice wine vinegar

¼ cup good soy sauce

1-inch piece of fresh ginger, peeled and finely grated

½ teaspoon red pepper flakes

1 teaspoon superfine sugar

juice of 1 lime

In a bowl, dissolve the salt in ¾ cup hand-hot water and mix with the flour to form a soft dough. Turn onto a well-floured surface and knead for at least 5 minutes until the dough is very smooth and slightly springy. Divide into 8 balls (or 16 if you wish to serve as a party snack), brush very lightly with oil, put in a bowl covered with a damp kitchen towel, and set aside to rest for 30 minutes.

Meanwhile, mix the rice wine vinegar in a bowl with the soy sauce, ginger, red pepper flakes, sugar, and lime juice, then divide into individual bowls ready to serve. Set aside.

On a floured surface, roll out each ball into a thin rectangle about 4 x 12 inches. Brush with sesame oil and sprinkle with the scallion and five-spice powder, if using. Starting at the long end, roll the dough into a cigar shape, brush the inside with a little more sesame oil, then roll into a snail shape and tuck under the ends. Press lightly with your hands to flatten the spiral. Roll it out very gently into an ultra-thin pancake. You should still see the coils. Roll gently to retain flakiness and turn often to avoid making holes in the pancakes. Cover the prepared pancakes with a damp cloth. Repeat with the remaining dough.

Heat a nonstick frying pan over medium heat and brush with sunflower oil. When the oil is shimmering, slip the first pancake into the hot pan. It should sizzle and not burn. Cook for 2 minutes or until golden, shaking the pan gently. Flip over and cook for another 2 minutes or until golden. Drain on a plate covered with paper towels. Repeat with the remaining pancake coils. Serve warm with the dipping sauce.

Kuku Sibzamini

PERSIAN-STYLE SAFFRON AND SWEET POTATO PANCAKE

A Persian egg-based frittata, *kuku*, is eaten at New Year in Iran. The herbs symbolize rebirth, and the eggs promise fertility and happiness for the year to come. When made with potato, it is called *kuku sibzamini*. I've long adored sweet potato, and using it here gives the pancake a slightly different, richer flavor. I've scented it with saffron, which raises the dish to another level of intense flavor. The addition of walnuts for an interesting crunch, and tiny Iranian barberries for a refreshing sour zing, is traditional and adds surprise. I make one large *kuku sibzamini* and my preference is to serve it warm or at room temperature, cut into wedges with cool yogurt mixed with cucumber and lots of fresh mint, dill, and parsley.

PREP 15 mins

COOK 30 mins

TOTAL 45 mins

DIETARY

GLUTEN-FREE

MAKES

1 x 10IN,
SERVES 6 AS A SNACK,
2 AS A MAIN MEAL

1 pound sweet potatoes, unpeeled and cut into quarters
½ teaspoon saffron threads
3 large eggs
2 tablespoons all-purpose flour
2 teaspoons baking powder
½ teaspoon baking soda
1 garlic clove, crushed
a large bunch of parsley, finely chopped
a large bunch of mint, finely chopped
a large bunch of dill, finely chopped
¾ ounce chervil and tarragon (optional), finely chopped

½ cup walnuts, finely chopped
½ cup barberries or cranberries, soaked, rinsed, and dried on paper towels
sunflower oil or canola oil
sea salt and freshly ground black pepper

FOR THE YOGURT SAUCE
½ cup Greek yogurt
½ cucumber peeled and diced
a large handful each of fresh parsley, mint, and dill, leaves finely chopped
rose petals, to decorate (optional)

Bring a pan of salted water to a boil and cook the potato for 10 to 15 minutes until fork-tender. Cool a little, remove the skins, then mash. Crush the saffron using a mortar and pestle, then put it in a small bowl and add 1 tablespoon boiling water. Let soak.

Put the eggs in a bowl and sift in the flour, baking powder, and baking soda. Add the garlic, herbs, saffron in its liquid, walnuts, and barberries. Season with salt and pepper, then stir in the mashed sweet potatoes.

Heat a little oil in a large, heavy frying pan over medium heat until it begins to sizzle, then reduce the heat and pour in all the *kuku* batter. Cook for 1 minute, then loosen the kuku around the edges. Cover with a lid and continue to cook over low heat for 20 to 30 minutes or until the *kuku* is just set and still fluffy within. Cut into wedges.

To make the sauce, put the yogurt in a bowl and add the cucumber and herbs. Season with salt and pepper, then mix together well. Pour the yogurt sauce over the *kuku* and garnish with dried rose petals for an optional added flourish, if you like.

Main Meals

Farçous

SWISS CHARD PANCAKES WITH LEMON BERBERE BUTTER

Farçou comes from Aveyron in southwest France, although it is a popular staple throughout the region. It has the texture of a thick crêpe and tastes hugely healthy as it is loaded with greens, specifically Swiss chard, plus masses of herbs (usually parsley and chives) and garlic. As an accompaniment, I created a lemon berbere—an Ethiopian hot spice that is available ready blended (containing chile, garlic, ginger, cardamom, clove, and fenugreek)—butter accompaniment. The French generally serve *farçous* as a robust main meal—either as small fritters or a large frying-pan-sized *farçou*—with salad. I recommend one of bitter leaves, Roquefort, and walnuts to stay with the southwest French flavors. The batter will keep in the fridge for two days. Cooked *farçous* even taste good cold the next day if any are leftover. They also freeze well, wrapped in wax paper for up to one month.

PREP   10 mins
*plus 1 hour chilling

COOK   20 mins

TOTAL   40 mins

DIETARY

USE GLUTEN-FREE
ALL-PURPOSE FLOUR

MAKES

16 x 3IN,
SERVES 4

FOR THE LEMON BERBERE BUTTER
7 tablespoons unsalted butter, at room temperature
1 teaspoon berbere spice mix (available online)
zest of 1 lemon and 2 tablespoons lemon juice

FOR THE FARÇOUS
1¼ cups all-purpose flour, sifted
6 scallions, finely chopped
1 cup low-fat milk
2 large eggs
8 Swiss chard leaves, tougher stems discarded, finely chopped
2 garlic cloves, crushed
a small bunch of flat-leaf parsley, finely chopped
10 chives, finely chopped
sprinkle of freshly grated nutmeg
salt and freshly ground black pepper
sunflower oil or canola oil

To make the berbere butter, cream the butter in a small bowl. Add the spice, lemon zest and juice, season with salt and pepper, and mix well. Form into a long roll, then cover with plastic wrap and put it in the freezer for 15 minutes or in the fridge for 1 hour to firm up.

Preheat the oven to 225°F, line a baking sheet with foil, and put it in the oven to keep the *farçous* warm while you make them.

Put the flour, scallions, milk, and eggs in a blender or food processor pulse-blend to make a batter. Add the Swiss chard and garlic and process briefly so there are still some longish strands of green leaves. Pour into a bowl and stir in the herbs, nutmeg, and salt and pepper.

Place a large nonstick frying pan over medium heat. Smear generously with oil using paper towels and heat until hot enough that a droplet of batter sizzles. Add 2 tablespoons of the batter to make small *farçous*, or you can make several pan-sized ones instead. Cook for 3 minutes or until lightly browned underneath and turning frilly at the edges. Flip over and cook for another 2 minutes. Keep warm in the oven and repeat with the remaining batter, adding more oil to the pan as necessary. Serve with the lemon berbere butter.

Crespelle

BAKED SPINACH AND RICOTTA CRESPELLE WITH TOMATO SAUCE

This is a truly comforting dish that features a classic Italian combination of spinach (do use fresh), ricotta, and tomato. The crespelles should really be as thin as cannelloni. The velvety sauce thickens as it cooks.

PREP 30 mins

COOK 40 mins

TOTAL 70 mins

MAKES

8 x 10IN,
SERVES 4

1 cup all-purpose flour
3 large eggs
¾ cup low-fat milk
3 tablespoons melted butter
1 to 2 tablespoons oil

FOR THE TOMATO SAUCE
1 tablespoon extra virgin olive oil
1 red onion, finely chopped
1 garlic clove, crushed
1 x 14-ounce can chopped tomatoes
1 teaspoon superfine sugar
½ cup basil leaves, shredded

FOR THE FILLING
1 tablespoon extra virgin olive oil
1 red onion, finely chopped
1 garlic clove, crushed
12 ounces spinach
9 ounces ricotta
zest of ½ lemon
1 ounce anchovies in olive oil, chopped
½ cup Parmesan, grated
½ teaspoon freshly grated nutmeg
sea salt and freshly ground black
pepper

To make the tomato sauce, heat the oil in a small pan and cook the onion for 5 minutes or until soft. Add the garlic and cook for 1 minute. Add the tomatoes and sugar and cook for 15 to 20 minutes until thick. Season to taste, then add the basil.

Meanwhile, to make the filling, heat the oil in a saucepan over medium heat, add the onion, and cook for 5 minutes or until soft. Add the garlic, cook for another 1 minute, then add the spinach. Reduce the heat, cover, and cook gently for 2 minutes to wilt the spinach. Pour into a strainer over a bowl and press out any excess liquid. Transfer to another bowl, cool slightly, and add the ricotta, lemon zest, anchovies, ⅓ cup of the Parmesan, and the nutmeg. Season to taste.

While the sauce is cooking, put the flour and eggs in a large bowl and season with salt. Gradually whisk in the milk and butter until you have a smooth batter with the consistency of heavy cream. Pour into a glass measuring cup. Preheat the oven to 350°F.

Heat a large nonstick frying pan over medium–high heat and add 1 tablespoon oil. Spread evenly with paper towels. Pour about 5 tablespoons of batter into the center of the pan and immediately swirl it around so that it evenly covers the whole of the bottom. Cook for 2 minutes, or until the top is set and the base is golden. Flip over and cook for 1 minute. Transfer to a plate. Repeat with the remaining batter, adding more oil to the pan as necessary. Put 2 tablespoons of the filling at the base of each pancake and roll up. Arrange the pancakes seam-side down in an oiled ovenproof dish. Spoon over the sauce, sprinkle with the remaining Parmesan, and bake for 20 to 25 minutes until bubbling hot and a little crisp on top.

Arepas de Choclo

WITH BLACK BEANS, SPICY AVOCADO, MANGO, AND TOMATO SALSA

These Colombian and Venezuelan pancakes are usually made from cornmeal and stuffed with cheese or served as a savory "sandwich," brimming with chicken and avocado, chorizo, plantain, or black beans. The Venezuelans favor a thicker, rounded, palm-shaped arepa, split open and filled, whereas the Colombians prefer larger, floppier arepas that fold around fillings. Ideally, use a yellow or white masarepa maize flour that is precooked (found in Colombian and Caribbean stores; a make called PAN Harina is popular). If you can't find it, instant polenta works too and gives a rather appealing coarser texture, although the arepas don't end up so fluffy and thick.

PREP 30 mins

COOK 20 mins

TOTAL 50 mins

DIETARY

POLENTA AND MASAREPA ARE BOTH GLUTEN-FREE

MAKES

8 x 4in, SERVES 4

1¼ cups corn kernels, fresh or frozen, cooked

1 cup low-fat milk

1 tablespoon unsalted butter

7 ounces store-bought polenta

1 teaspoon superfine sugar

1 cup mozzarella, grated

small bunch of cilantro, chopped

½ green chile, seeded and finely chopped

butter or oil, for cooking

FOR THE FILLING

1 x 14-ounce can black beans, drained

1 teaspoon paprika

1 garlic clove, crushed

1 tablespoon avocado oil or olive oil

⅔ cup sour cream

3 tablespoons chopped cilantro

FOR THE SALSA

14 ounces tomatoes, chopped

2 avocados, chopped

1 mango, chopped

1 green chile, seeded and chopped

zest and juice of 1 lime

8 radishes, finely sliced

a small bunch of cilantro, chopped

2 tablespoons olive oil

sea salt and freshly ground pepper

Preheat the oven to 225°F and heat a plate to keep the arepas warm.

Put the corn in a blender and add the milk. Pulse until the corn is coarsely ground. Pour into a saucepan over medium–high heat and add the butter. Heat until the milk is just boiling. Cool a little. Put the polenta in a bowl and mix in the sugar and ½ teaspoon salt. Add the mozzarella, cilantro, and chile. Stir in the milk mixture (the polenta will absorb some of the liquid). Season. You'll have a thick pancake batter, not a pouring batter.

Mix the filling ingredients in a bowl. Mix the salsa ingredients together and season well.

Melt a small pat of butter in a large frying pan. Spoon in 3 tablespoons of batter to make a pancake about 5 inches in diameter and 1¼-inch thick. Press down gently using a spatula and cook for 2 to 3 minutes, until golden. Flip over and cook for 5 to 7 minutes. Keep warm. Repeat with the remaining batter, adding more butter to the pan as necessary. When ready, split an arepa through the center without cutting right through, then fill with the bean mixture or pile beans on top of the arepa. Serve with the salsa.

Hoppers

I first came across these at Hoppers, the massively popular Soho restaurant owned by
the Sethi family, where lines form at each service for these pancakes. I was completely entranced by their
filigree-thin, curved bowl-shape, and the egg nestling in the middle.
Hoppers are Sri Lanka's favorite breakfast, and taste distinctively tangy and sweetly rich because they are fermented
overnight and made with coconut milk and rice flour. They're gluten-free too. Despite being told
that they are fiendishly hard to perfect, I was determined to master cooking them myself. The bowl shape comes
from using a special hopper or *appam* pan. It's a good idea to locate an inexpensive nonstick one if you can—I found
one at an Asian specialty shop. They're like small woks with outward-sloping sides and should come
with a lid. Otherwise, a small nonstick wok or high-sided omelet pan with a lid works well. At Hoppers,
they dip half an onion into sunflower oil and rub it around the hopper pan, which works most effectively in making
the hoppers easy to remove. I would advise having at least one practice run when making hoppers before inviting
guests over. For a more substantial meal, serve with a Sri Lankan chicken curry. I have given here a coconut
sambol and an onion sambol alternative plus kiri hodi, a spinach "gravy."

PREP 45 mins

* *plus 30 mins and overnight resting*

COOK 30 mins

TOTAL 75 mins

DIETARY

RICE FLOUR IS
GLUTEN-FREE

MAKES

8 x 8IN,
SERVES 4

1 package fast-acting yeast
1 x 14-ounce can coconut milk,
shaken well
1 teaspoon superfine sugar
1¼ cups brown rice flour, sifted, plus
extra if needed
coconut oil, for cooking
8 large eggs
wedges of lime, chili sauce, and sprigs
of fresh cilantro, to serve

FOR THE COCONUT SAMBOL
1 green chile, finely chopped
1 shallot, finely sliced
2 tablespoons cilantro, finely chopped
2 teaspoons bonito flakes (optional)
2½ cups grated coconut, (you can use
fresh coconut pieces)
zest and juice of 1 lime
salt and freshly ground black pepper

FOR THE ONION SAMBOL
4 cardamom pods
4 tablespoons sunflower or canola oil
4 whole cloves
1½-inch piece of cinnamon stick
1¼ pounds red onions, finely sliced
1 green chile, finely chopped
1 tablespoon lime juice
2 teaspoons sugar, or to taste

FOR THE KIRI HODI
1 red onion, sliced
2 garlic cloves, crushed
1-inch piece of fresh ginger, grated
1 teaspoon ground turmeric
1 teaspoon ground fenugreek seeds
1-inch piece of cinnamon stick
1 green chile, finely chopped
6 to 8 fresh curry leaves, to taste
1 x 14-ounce can coconut milk,
shaken well
4½ ounces baby spinach leaves, chopped
juice of ½ lime

Put the yeast in a bowl, add ½ cup of the coconut milk and the sugar, and whisk to combine. Let stand for 30 minutes or until the batter begins to bubble, then add the remaining coconut milk and ½ cup warm water. Put the rice flour in a large bowl. Make a well in the center and pour in the yeasty coconut liquid. Whisk until smooth to make a thin batter. Add a little more warm water if necessary. Cover the bowl with plastic wrap and leave at room temperature overnight.

The next day, to make the coconut sambol, put the chile in a blender and add the shallot, cilantro, and bonito flakes, if using, and 1 teaspoon salt. Blend to a smooth paste. Pour into a bowl, then add the grated coconut, a good grinding of black pepper, and the lime zest and juice. Stir well, then cover and chill.

To make the onion sambol, bash the cardamom pods in a mortar and pestle. Heat the oil in a frying pan and add the cardamom, cloves, and cinnamon. When the spices smell aromatic, add the onions, chile, and 1 teaspoon salt, then cook over medium–low heat for 30 to 40 minutes, stirring occasionally to ensure the onions don't burn. Stir in the lime juice and sugar to taste, then cook until the sugar has dissolved. Check the seasoning and remove from the heat.

Put all the ingredients for the kiri hodi, except the spinach and lime juice, in a saucepan set over medium heat and simmer for 15 minutes or until the onions have softened and the sauce has thickened. Add the spinach and stir to wilt. Remove from the heat. Season to taste with salt and add the lime juice. Remove the cinnamon stick and curry leaves. Keep warm.

Stir the hopper batter and add 1 teaspoon salt and a little more warm water to loosen it if it is too thick. It should be the consistency of half-and-half. Heat a hopper pan over medium–high heat, then add 1 tablespoon coconut oil and tip the pan to coat it in the oil, removing any excess using paper towels. Working quickly, add a ladleful of batter to the pan, then immediately hold the pan by its handles and swirl it in a circular motion to make a thin pancake that coats the base and sides of the pan. A hopper should have a thin, lacy layer of batter sticking to the sides with a slightly thicker layer in the center. If the hopper batter doesn't stick to the sides of the pan, whisk in a few extra tablespoons of rice flour for the next round, or use a spoon to add extra batter to the sides. When the outside of the hopper is just beginning to set, crack an egg into the center and cover the pan with a lid. Cook for 2 minutes or until the egg white has set and the hopper is crisp and golden. The egg yolk should still be slightly creamy in the middle.

Use a palette knife or spatula to carefully ease the hopper from the pan and lift it out. Serve the hoppers immediately, topped with the coconut or onion sambol and the kiri hodi, a wedge of lime, and some fresh cilantro. For those who like an extra kick, have chili sauce ready to offer on the side. Repeat with the remaining batter, adding more oil to the pan as necessary, a teaspoon at a time. The hoppers can be reheated for 4 to 5 minutes in an oven preheated to 225°F on a baking sheet lined with parchment paper.

Chennai Dosa

POTATO, CAULIFLOWER, AND CASHEW CURRY WITH COCONUT CHUTNEY

The dramatic crisp dosa I adore at the southern Indian restaurants in Tooting are quite a feat to pull off at home, because they need to be prepared over several days and require grinding and fermenting rice and *urad dhal* (black split peas). I like pancakes to be more of a spur-of-the-moment decision and I asked my friend, Romy Gill, chef-proprietor of Romy's Kitchen near Bristol, England if she could suggest an easier alternative. This chennai dosa is her recipe with a few tweaks. It uses semolina flour, rice flour, and buttermilk. It still takes practice to get the batter ultra-thin and crisp, although it is well worth the effort. The potato, cauliflower, and cashew curry is a family favorite adapted from a Sophie Grigson recipe and it makes this into a substantial meal. Simpler coconut potatoes would also make a good accompaniment. I adore fresh coconut chutney, although I admit that I cheated and used fresh coconut chunks rather than smashing my own coconut.

PREP  40 mins

* plus 30 mins resting

COOK 40 mins

TOTAL 80 mins

DIETARY

USE GLUTEN-FREE
SELF-RISING FLOUR

MAKES

8 x 10in,
SERVES 4

¾ cup semolina flour
¾ cup rice flour, plus extra if needed
3 tablespoons self-rising flour
1 green chile, seeded and chopped
½ teaspoon red pepper flakes
1¼-inch piece of fresh ginger, peeled and grated
1 red onion, chopped
5 fresh curry leaves
a handful of cilantro leaves, chopped
1 teaspoon cumin seeds, crushed
salt and freshly ground black pepper
2 cups buttermilk
sunflower oil or canola oil, for cooking

FOR THE POTATO, CAULIFLOWER, AND CASHEW CURRY
1 large onion, coarsely chopped
2 garlic cloves, finely chopped
1-inch piece of fresh ginger, peeled and grated
1 dried chile, seeded and chopped
1 teaspoon ground turmeric
1 tablespoon ground cumin
3 tablespoons sunflower oil or canola oil
1 pound potatoes, peeled and cut into small cubes

½ cauliflower, broken into small florets
1 tablespoon lemon juice
¾ cup cashews
3 tablespoons coarsely chopped cilantro leaves

FOR THE COCONUT CHUTNEY
1 tablespoon sunflower oil or canola oil
1 teaspoon black mustard seeds
4 dried curry leaves
1 green chile, seeded and chopped
¾-inch piece of fresh ginger, peeled and chopped
zest and juice of 1 lime
1 cup fresh coconut, diced into small pieces

FOR THE GARAM MASALA
1 tablespoon cumin seeds
1 tablespoon coriander seeds
1 teaspoon fennel seeds
8 green cardamom pods
1 teaspoon black peppercorns
2 bay leaves
1 teaspoon ground cinnamon

Sift all the flours into a large bowl and add the green chile and red pepper flakes, ginger, onion, curry leaves, cilantro leaves, cumin seeds, and a little salt, then mix well. Gradually whisk in the buttermilk to make a thin batter without any lumps. Add 2 tablespoons of water if it seems too thick, or if it seems too thin add a little more rice flour to thicken it. Rest for 30 minutes.

Meanwhile, to make the curry, put the onion into the smallest bowl of a food processor and add the garlic, ginger, chile, turmeric, cumin, 1 teaspoon salt, and 2 tablespoons water, then process to a paste. Heat 2 tablespoons sunflower oil in a wide, heavy-bottomed saucepan over medium heat and add the spice paste. Cook, stirring constantly, for 3 minutes.

Add the potatoes and cauliflower and stir to coat with the paste. Add ½ cup water and the lemon juice and bring to a boil. Reduce to a simmer over low heat and cook, covered, for 10 to 15 minutes until the vegetables are tender but not collapsing. If there is still a lot of liquid, take the lid off and allow most of the water to cook off.

Meanwhile, put 1 tablespoon sunflower oil in a small frying pan over medium–high heat and pan-fry the cashews until lightly brown. Stir into the curry and cook for 1 to 2 minutes until blended.

To make the chutney, heat a small frying pan with the oil and pan-fry the mustard seeds and curry leaves until they start to sizzle. Transfer to a blender and add the chile, ginger, lime zest and juice, coconut, and a little salt. Process and add ½ cup hot water to make a thick paste.

To make the garam masala, put the cumin seeds in a small, heavy frying pan and add the coriander and fennel seeds, cardamom pods, and black peppercorns. Heat over low heat for 2 to 3 minutes until they begin to smell aromatic. Remove from the heat, cool a little, then add the bay leaves and cinnamon. Crush the mixture using a mortar and pestle. This will make more than you need, but it is a useful mix to have on standby. Set aside.

Preheat the oven to 225°F and warm a plate to keep the dosas warm while you make them. Remove from the oven and turn off the oven. To cook the dosas, heat a nonstick frying pan over medium–high heat and add 1 tablespoon sunflower oil. Spread oil evenly with paper towels. Pour a ladleful of batter into the pan, and either immediately swirl it around so that the batter spreads out evenly and thinly or use a circular motion with a wooden crêpe spreader, spreading thinly from the center to the edges.

Add 1 teaspoon of the oil on the top of the dosa to make it more crisp. Cook for 1 to 2 minutes, making sure that the base is golden. Flip over and cook for 1 to 2 minutes until golden. Transfer the dosa to a warm plate. Keep warm with a clean kitchen towel over the plate while cooking the remaining dosas. Repeat with the remaining batter, adding more oil to the pan as necessary.

Sprinkle the garam masala mix and the cilantro leaves over the curry. Serve with the dosa and coconut chutney.

Okonomiyaki

SHRIMP, SPICY TAMARIND SAUCE, AND JAPANESE MAYO

Okonomiyaki-ya restaurants are hugely popular in Japan, often offering the option to cook one's own over a *teppan*, or hotplate. The name means "as you like it, grilled," so there really is not one defining recipe. They are made with *okonomiyaki* flour, dashi stock, eggs, and an obligatory cabbage filling, plus whatever you have on hand, whether it is seafood, pork, or bacon. The Japanese, however, are quite strict about their garnishes, which should include a special sweet-and-sour condiment like brown sauce, Japanese *kewpie* mayo, seaweed powder, and bonito flakes that dance on the top of the hot *okonomiyaki* and impart plenty of umami richness. All are widely available at specialty Japanese stores. This recipe is *okonomiyaki* Osaka-style, where all the ingredients are mixed together rather than layered and served on top of fried noodles as in Hiroshima.

PREP  15 *mins*

COOK 10 *mins*

TOTAL 25 *mins*

DIETARY

USE A RICE-FLOUR-BASED OKONOMIYAKI FLOUR

MAKES

2 x 10IN SERVES 2

1½ cups okonomiyaki flour
¾ cup water or half water/half dashi
½ pointy cabbage, finely shredded
4 scallions, finely chopped
7 ounces raw jumbo shrimp, thinly sliced pork belly, thinly sliced unsmoked bacon, or tofu
1¼-inch piece of fresh ginger, grated
2 ounces tenkasu tempura batter balls (optional)

2 large eggs, beaten
peanut oil, for cooking

TO SERVE

Japanese kewpie mayonnaise
okonomiyaki sauce, bought or homemade (see below)
2 tablespoons dried bonito flakes
2 tablespoons aonori seaweed
2 tablespoons pickled ginger

Preheat the oven to 225°F and warm a plate to keep the *okonomiyaki* warm while you make them. In a large bowl, mix together the flour and ¾ cup water. Add the cabbage to the batter, then the scallions, shrimp, ginger, and tenkasu balls, if using. Add the eggs and mix everything together gently.

Heat 1 tablespoon oil in a lidded frying pan over medium heat. Pour in half the *okonomiyaki* mixture and flatten it with a spatula to form a round pancake about ½-inch thick. Cook for 5 minutes or until golden, covering the pan with the lid to ensure it is evenly cooked. Flip over and cook, again covered, for another 5 minutes. Keep warm. Repeat with the remaining mixture. Serve with mayo and *okonomiyaki* sauce drizzled over in ribbons and bonito flakes, aonori seaweed, and pickled ginger scattered decorously.

To make *okonomiyaki* sauce, put ½ cup dashi stock in a pan over medium–high heat. Add 5 tablespoons Worcestershire sauce, 2 tablespoons ketchup, 2 tablespoons tomato paste, 2 tablespoons tamarind paste, 2 tablespoons dark soy sauce, 2 tablespoons apple juice, 1 teaspoon brown sugar, and 1 teaspoon honey. Bring to a boil, stirring well to prevent it from burning on the base of the pan. Put 2 teaspoons cornstarch in a bowl and stir in 3 teaspoons cold water. Add the cornstarch mixture a little at a time to the hot mixture, stirring well. Cook over low heat for 5 minutes or until the sauce has thickened to the consistency of a glossy ketchup. Let cool, then transfer to a glass measuring cup. Store in the fridge until ready to use.

Banh Xeo

This is a crisp and lacy bright-yellow pancake from Vietnam that is far more substantial than a spring roll. Its name means "sizzling cake," derived from the impressively loud sizzling sound the rice flour and coconut milk batter makes when it is dropped into the hot pan. *Bang xeo* is traditionally served with both pork and shrimp, although I've made a lighter version with just shrimp and added extra crisp vegetables. For a vegan version, add fine strips of mooli and carrots and leave out the shrimp altogether. *Banh xeo* is immensely pleasing, with complex layers of flavor, texture, and freshness. The distinction between a good and a brilliant *banh xeo* is in the thinness and crispness of the batter. I also like that it is usually eaten wrapped in lettuce leaves with masses of fragrant herbs.

PREP 25 mins

plus 30 mins or overnight resting

COOK 10 mins

TOTAL 45 mins

DIETARY

BATTER IS GLUTEN-FREE AND VEGAN

MAKES

6 x 10IN, SERVES 3

1¼ cups brown rice flour
½ teaspoon salt
1 teaspoon ground turmeric
1¼ cups coconut milk
⅔ cup warm water
3 tablespoons peanut oil, or sunflower oil or canola oil, for cooking

FOR THE DIPPING SAUCE
2½ tablespoons lime juice
1½ tablespoons sesame oil
1 tablespoon brown sugar
1 tablespoon rice wine vinegar
1 tablespoon sweet soy sauce (kecap manis)
¾-inch piece of fresh ginger, peeled and grated
1 small Thai red chile, or to taste, finely chopped
1 garlic clove, crushed

½ teaspoon salt
¼ cup warm water

FOR THE FILLING
3 tablespoons peanut oil, or sunflower oil or canola oil
1 onion, finely sliced
⅔ cup shiitake mushrooms, finely sliced
1¼ cups snow peas, sliced into thin strips
5½ ounces raw shrimp
5½ ounces bean sprouts
3 scallions, diagonally sliced

TO SERVE
1 head Romaine lettuce
½ cup cilantro leaves
½ cup mint leaves
½ cup Thai basil leaves

Preheat the oven to 225°F and warm a plate to keep the pancakes warm while you make them. Put the rice flour in a bowl and add the salt and turmeric. Slowly pour in the coconut milk, whisking to ensure there are no lumps, until you have a batter the consistency of half-and-half. Add up to ⅔ cup warm water to thin the batter, if necessary. Set aside to rest for at least 30 minutes or overnight.

To make the dipping sauce, put all the ingredients in a bowl with ¼ cup warm water and whisk together, ensuring the sugar is dissolved. Set aside.

To make the filling, heat 2 tablespoons of the oil in a large frying pan, add the onion and mushrooms, and cook gently until the onion softens and the mushrooms start to brown. Add the snow peas and stir to warm through but retain their crispness. Remove from the pan.Heat the remaining oil in the frying pan over medium heat. Add the shrimp and cook for 1 to 2 minutes until pink, then stir in the mushroom mixture. Keep warm with a lid over very low heat.

To cook the pancakes, heat a large, heavy frying pan over medium heat and add 1 tablespoon oil. Spread evenly with paper towels so that the oil covers the base very lightly. Turn the heat up to high and, when the oil is very hot, pour in ¼ cup of the batter, and immediately swirl it around so that the batter spreads out to the edges of the pan. The edges can be thinner than the center of the *banh xeo* to encourage them to crisp.

Add a small handful of the mushroom mixture with some bean sprouts and scallion. Cover the pan with a lid and cook for 3 minutes or until the *banh xeo* turns very crisp. It should be golden at the edges and coming away from the pan. Remove the lid and use a spatula to fold one half of the pancake over the other. Transfer to the warmed plate and keep warm in the oven. Repeat the process until you have six pancakes—the batter may need to be rewhisked after each *banh xeo* to ensure there are no lumps.

Serve the *banh xeo* with plenty of lettuce leaves, cilantro, mint, and Thai basil with the dipping sauce in small bowls on the side. The traditional way to eat *banh xeo* is to take a lettuce leaf, pile some herbs onto it, then break off a piece of the pancake and place it inside the leaf. Roll it up like a spring roll and dip it into the sauce.

Galettes de Sarrasin

LEEKS, MERGUEZ SAUSAGE, AND HARISSA YOGURT

Brittany is home to savory crêpes made with buckwheat flour called galettes de sarrasin. I remember many a Breton childhood holiday full of galettes. My favorite was always the galette complet, with a whole egg cracked into the galette plus some spinach and folded in on itself like an envelope. Buckwheat flour is easy to find now. I usually make half and half with all-purpose flour, however, as buckwheat alone can taste rather dense, although I do like its nutty, toasty flavor. Bretons often add a splash of beer to the batter. Traditionally, the first galette is a disaster and either discarded or cut up and put into soup, so don't be disheartened.

Aside from the classics, including ham and Gruyère, which is satisfyingly gooey, I like something punchy, such as caramelized leeks with grilled merguez sausages and a good dollop of yogurt with harissa. The galettes can be prepared with sweet fillings too. A classic is apples and salted caramel sauce.

PREP 30 mins
plus 2 hours or overnight resting

COOK 10 mins

TOTAL 40 mins

DIETARY

USE GLUTEN-FREE FLOUR AND SOY MILK OR ALMOND MILK

MAKES

8 x 10IN (BEFORE FOLDING), SERVES 4

1⅔ cups buckwheat flour

⅓ cup all-purpose flour

½ teaspoon fine sea salt

2 large eggs

2 cups low-fat milk

2 tablespoons rose harissa

a handful of fresh mint leaves, torn

1 cup Greek yogurt

8 merguez sausages

sunflower oil or canola oil, for cooking

green salad, to serve

FOR THE CARAMELIZED LEEKS

2 tablespoons extra virgin olive oil

2 tablespoons butter

4 leeks, cut into 2-inch pieces

2 tablespoon brown sugar

Sift the flours and salt into a large mixing bowl and make a little well in the center. Break the eggs into the well and whisk them gradually into the flour in a circular motion.

Pour the milk in slowly, whisking all the time. Add 2 cups of cold water, still whisking. Cover and put in the fridge for at least 2 hours, or ideally overnight.

Meanwhile, to make the caramelized leeks, heat the oil and butter in a pan, add the leeks, and cook for 10 minutes to wilt, then add the sugar. Add enough water to cover and cook for 10 minutes or until the water has evaporated. Set aside.

Stir the rose harissa and mint leaves into the yogurt, then set aside.

Take the batter out of the fridge and rewhisk, as some of the flour will have settled at the bottom of the bowl. Preheat the broiler and cook the merguez for 10 to 15 minutes or until cooked through. Keep warm.

Preheat the oven to 225°F and put a large baking sheet in the oven to keep the galettes warm while you make them.

Heat a large frying pan over high heat. When very hot, smear on sunflower oil using paper towels to leave a shimmer of oil on the pan. Pour a ladleful of batter into the pan and immediately swirl it around so that the batter spreads out into an even circle. Reduce the heat to medium and cook for 2 minutes or until golden underneath. Flip over and cook for another 2 minutes or until golden.

Put the caramelized leek and merguez, chopped into chunks, in the middle of the galette. Fold the galette: the traditional way is to fold in the four sides to make a square package. If there is lots of filling, just fold two sides in.

Keep the filled galettes warm in the baking sheet in the oven and repeat with the remaining batter, adding more oil to the pan as necessary. Serve with harissa yogurt and accompany with a green salad and, preferably, generous amounts of sparkling cider.

Cornmeal Chorizo Pancakes

CABRALES BLUE CHEESE SAUCE, TOMATO, AND LIME SALSA

Asturias is an astoundingly dramatic green and wild region of Spain, which is still, inexplicably, little touched by tourism. I remember having a similar cornmeal pancake to this on the wooden veranda of a village café with stunning views of the Picos de Europa mountains. The pancake is light yet rich with a grainy sweetness from the cornmeal, and the chorizo adds a spicy note and a chewy texture. Cabrales is an exceptionally strong artisan blue cheese produced only in Asturias and available at specialty Spanish stores (or you can substitute Gorgonzola), giving this dish serious punch. It has to be experienced. The fresh tomato salsa adds a refreshing antidote.

PREP 20 mins

COOK 15 mins

TOTAL 35 mins

DIETARY

USE GLUTEN-FREE CORNMEAL

MAKES

12 X 4IN,
SERVES 4

¾ cup sour cream
1 large egg
¾ cup cornmeal or maize meal
½ cup all-purpose flour
1 teaspoon baking powder
½ teaspoon baking soda
pinch of salt
7 ounces cooked chorizo, finely chopped
4 tablespoons finely chopped parsley
olive oil, for cooking

sea salt and freshly ground black pepper

FOR THE TOMATO AND LIME SALSA
1¾ cups cherry tomatoes, quartered
zest of 1 lime and juice of ½ lime

FOR THE CABRALES SAUCE
¾ cup half-and-half
7 ounces cabrales or gorgonzola cheese, chopped (about 1¾ cups)

Preheat the oven to 225°F and warm a plate for the pancakes.

To make the tomato and lime salsa, stir all the ingredients together in a bowl. Set aside.

For the pancakes, whisk together the sour cream and egg in a medium bowl using a hand mixer. Put the cornmeal in a large bowl and sift in the flour, baking powder, baking soda, and salt. Mix together using a wooden spoon. Stir in the sour cream mixture thoroughly to ensure there are no lumps. Add the chorizo and parsley and a good grinding of pepper.

Heat a large, nonstick frying pan over medium–high heat, then add 1 tablespoon oil and spread it thinly over the pan using paper towels. Add 2 tablespoons of batter to make each pancake about 4 inches in size and flatten the batter quickly. Cook for 2 to 3 minutes or until golden. Flip over and cook for another 1 to 2 minutes. Keep warm in the oven. Repeat with the remaining batter, adding more oil to the pan as necessary.

Meanwhile, heat the half-and-half in a pan over medium heat, add the cabrales, and allow it to melt slowly. Season with pepper to taste. There is no need to add salt, as the cheese is quite salty.

To serve, pour the cabrales sauce over the chorizo pancakes and put the tomato and lime salsa on the side.

Jian Bing

Vendors are found in every neighborhood in China selling *jian bing*—one of China's favorite street breakfasts. It's long been a well-kept culinary secret. I've only recently come across self-taught Western pioneers bringing *jian bing* to America and Europe. Mee Mee Street Cart, owned by twins Melissa and Oliver Fu, who pop up in London and Manchester, produce the best I've ever tasted, so I was determined to make a version at home with the help of my Singaporean friend, Loretta Liu, chef-owner of Café On in London. What makes crisp-fried *jian bing* pancakes so appealing is the bold yin-and-yang contrasts of flavor and texture. It's like a firework of taste: the soft egg spread across the crêpe-thin pancake (made with millet flour, although traditionally mung bean flour is used) as it cooks; the puffy, crackly wonton skins; the zingy freshness of cilantro, cucumber, iceberg lettuce, and crunchy scallions; and the sweet-spicy-salty hit of hoisin and chili sauce. I decided to add Chinese five-spice duck as a nod to the Peking duck I so relish, making the *jian bing* substantial enough for a meal.

Jian bing has a longer history than almost any other Chinese street food. I'm intrigued by the legend that suggests they originated in Shandong Province during the Three Kingdoms Period (AD220–80), when military strategist, Zhuge Liang, had his soldiers cook batter on shields held over the fire after their woks were lost!

PREP	20 mins
COOK	45 mins
TOTAL	65 mins

DIETARY

USE GLUTEN FREE FLOUR, SOY MILK

MAKES

4 X 10IN (BEFORE FOLDING), SERVES 4

2 duck breasts
2 tablespoons Chinese five-spice powder
1 tablespoon sunflower oil or canola oil, plus extra for shallow frying
7-ounce jar of good hoisin sauce or yellow bean paste
½ cup sriracha chili sauce
8 wonton wrappers
4 large eggs
a large bunch of scallions, diagonally chopped

½ cucumber, peeled and cut into small sticks
½ iceberg lettuce, finely chopped
a large bunch of cilantro, leaves finely chopped

FOR THE BATTER
1¾ cups millet flour or all-purpose flour, or a mixture of both
½ cup milk or soy milk
sunflower oil or canola oil, for cooking

Preheat the oven to 350°F. Set a rack over a roasting pan. Pat the duck breasts dry with paper towels. Score the skin with a knife, then rub with the five-spice powder.

Put the duck skin-side down in a cold, heavy frying pan, then turn the heat to medium–high, add the oil, and cook for 6 to 8 minutes until crisp, pouring off the fat regularly. Seal the other side for 30 seconds. Put skin-side up on the prepared roasting pan and cook for 10 minutes for rare or 15 minutes for medium. Set aside to rest in a warm place for 10 minutes. Slice thinly.

Meanwhile, to make the batter, put the millet in a bowl and add the milk and ½ cup water. Use a hand mixer to make a thin batter the consistency of whipping cream. Add another splash of water, if necessary, to thin it.

In a separate bowl, mix the hoisin sauce and chili sauce. Slice the wonton wrappers into thin strips. Heat a deep, heavy frying pan or wok with sunflower oil to a depth of 1¼ inches and heat until very hot, about 350°F (test by dropping in one slice of wonton; it should bubble immediately). Fry the wonton strips in batches for 2 to 3 minutes until lightly golden and crisp, spreading them out in the pan so that they don't stick. Remove with a slotted spoon and drain on paper towels.

Heat a large, heavy, nonstick frying pan over medium heat. Add 1 tablespoon oil. Ladle a quarter of the batter into the pan, and either immediately swirl it around so that the batter spreads out to cover the entire pan or spread it evenly with a spatula. Cook for 1 to 2 minutes until golden on the base yet still white on the top and just beginning to firm up.

Show bravado and crack one whole egg straight onto the *jian bing* (as the street vendors would do) or beat 1 egg and pour it over the *jian bing*, then spread it evenly. Cook for 2 minutes or until the egg is just set. Flip over and cook the egg side for up to 30 seconds or until lightly golden. Flip back so that the egg side is on top.

On one half of the pancake add some scallion slices, cucumber sticks, iceberg lettuce, and 1 tablespoon chopped cilantro, then press firmly into the egg. On the other half, spread 3 tablespoons of the hoisin and chili sauce mix and top with slices of duck. Add crisp wonton strips on top of the duck and vegetables.

Flip the top third of the pancake down over the wonton strips and flip the base third of the pancake up, then fold it in half. Fold paper towels in half and use it to hold the *jian bing*. Serve immediately. Repeat with the remaining batter, adding more oil to the pan as necessary.

Panqueta

WITH SPICED BEEF, OLIVES, TOMATO, AND CHIMICHURRI

For a really hearty, meaty pancake, the Brazilians—who love their beef—have a truly comforting pancake dish based on ground beef, tomato, and olives that I have given extra punch with chimichurri. It is the sort of pancake I make when I need a metaphorical warm hug.

PREP   30 mins

COOK   40 mins

TOTAL   70 mins

DIETARY

USE GLUTEN-FREE FLOUR

MAKES

6 X 10IN, SERVES 4

FOR THE CHIMICHURRI
1 large bunch of flat-leaf parsley, leaves finely chopped
1 bunch cilantro, leaves finely chopped
2 garlic cloves, crushed
1 jalapeño chile, seeded and chopped
5 tablespoons red wine vinegar
juice of 1 lemon
5 tablespoons extra virgin olive oil

FOR THE PANQUETA
1 cup all-purpose flour, sifted
1 egg and 1 yolk, beaten
1 cup low-fat milk
3 tablespoons chopped oregano leaves
butter, for greasing
sea salt and freshly ground black pepper
sunflower or canola oil
green salad with bitter leaves, to serve

FOR THE BEEF AND TOMATO FILLING
2 tablespoons sunflower or canola oil
2 red onions, finely chopped
2 garlic cloves, crushed
1 green chile, seeded and finely chopped
1 teaspoon ground cumin
1 teaspoon ground coriander
1 pound ground beef
14 ounces tomato sauce or chopped tomatoes
2 tablespoons tomato paste
2 tablespoons balsamic vinegar
⅓ cup pitted green olives, chopped
3 tablespoons chopped parsley leaves
⅓ cup Parmesan, grated

To make the chimichurri, put all the ingredients in a bowl and mix them together, add sea salt to taste, and then set aside to macerate for 3 hours.

Grease a large ovenproof dish and set aside. Put the flour in a large bowl. Make a well in the center and add the beaten eggs. Gradually whisk in the milk using a hand mixer to form a smooth batter the consistency of half-and-half. Stir in the chopped oregano and season to taste. Allow the batter to rest for at least 30 minutes before cooking.

Preheat the oven to 225°F and heat a plate to keep the pancakes warm while you make them.

Meanwhile, to make the beef filling, heat the oil in a large saucepan. Add the onions and cook for 5 minutes or until soft and lightly golden. Stir in the garlic, chile, cumin, and cilantro, and cook for 3 minutes. Add the beef and stir well so that it browns thoroughly. Add the tomato sauce, tomato paste, and balsamic vinegar. Bring to a boil, then reduce the heat and simmer uncovered for 30 minutes. Add the olives and parsley and season with salt and pepper.

To make the pancakes, place a large nonstick crêpe pan over medium heat. Add a tablespoon of oil and tilt the pan to cover the base completely. When properly hot, pour in 1 ladleful of batter and cook for 1 minute or until just set and golden underneath. Flip over and cook for 30 seconds or until lightly golden. Put the pancakes on the warmed plate, interleaved with parchment paper. Repeat with the remaining batter, adding more oil to the pan as necessary. The batter should make at least eight pancakes.

Increase the oven temperature to 400°F and remove the warm pancakes from the oven. Pour a line of beef sauce across the lower bottom half of one pancake and fold the lower edge over the sauce to cover it. Roll up neatly and put in the buttered ovenproof dish. Repeat with remaining pancakes, arranging them in a single layer.

Top the pancakes with grated Parmesan, then bake for 10 minutes or until the cheese is bubbling and brown. Serve with plenty of chimichurri drizzled over the top, and a big green salad made with mustardy/bitter leaves.

Afternoon tea & Desserts

Aebleskiver

These utterly addictive pancakes are like crisp, light, fluffy donuts. They are traditionally eaten at Christmas in Denmark and served with mulled wine. To make them, you need a cast-iron *æbleskiver* pan that has five or seven spherical indentations. They are not expensive and are relatively easy to come by. Before using for the first time, the pan needs to be seasoned by oiling it all over and heating it in an extremely hot oven until nearly smoking for about 1 hour, then wiping off the excess oil. Mastering the art of turning an *æbleskiver* takes time, especially following the Danish tradition of using 2 knitting needles to do it! (I used wooden skewers instead.) It does take a certain amount of courage and belief to turn them while they are still soft but, believe me, the four quarter-turns I explain below are essential and the technique does work. Be careful not to have the heat too high.

PREP 20 mins

COOK 20 mins

TOTAL 40 mins

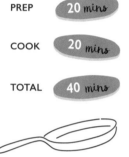

DIETARY

USE GLUTEN-FREE ALL-PURPOSE FLOUR

MAKES

16 x 2IN, SERVES 4

2 large egg whites
½ cup confectioners' sugar, sifted
1 teaspoon ground cinnamon
2 cups all-purpose flour
2 tablespoons superfine sugar
½ teaspoon baking soda
½ teaspoon salt

2 large egg yolks
2 cups buttermilk
4 tablespoons butter, melted
¾ cup sunflower oil or canola oil, for cooking
wild blueberry jam and whipped cream, to serve

Preheat the oven to 225°F and put in a rack on a baking sheet to keep the *æbleskiver* warm while you make them.

Put the egg whites in a clean, grease-free bowl and whisk until they form stiff peaks. Combine the confectioners' sugar and cinnamon for sprinkling later.

In another bowl, mix the flour, sugar, baking soda, salt, egg yolks, buttermilk, and melted butter. Carefully fold in the whisked egg whites. Make the *æbleskiver* immediately.

Place the *æbleskiver* pan over medium heat for a few minutes until it is really hot. Put 6 tablespoons sunflower oil in a small bowl. Using a heatproof pastry brush, liberally oil the base of each indentation. Pour about 2 tablespoons batter into each hole, filling it about three-quarters full. The batter should sizzle as it goes in. Cook for 1 to 2 minutes until the *æbleskiver* start to bubble on the surface and look as if they are starting to set around the edges. Immediately, turn a quarter-turn using a wooden skewer, a chopstick, or a fork. The technique is to slide the skewer between the edge of the pan and the cooked edge of the puffed pancake, then to move it so that it turns and the cooked part is lifted out of the pan. The uncooked batter will run into the base of the pan. Continue cooking a bit more, twisting the *æbleskiver* three further quarter-turns to form a puffy ball shape, allowing 1 to 2 minutes to cook each turn to a light golden color, and ensuring they don't burn. Repeat with the remaining batter, brushing each hole with a little more oil before cooking the next batch. Serve the *æbleskiver* rolled in the cinnamon sugar with blueberry jam and whipped cream.

Fluffy Coconut Pancakes

WITH THYME-BAKED APRICOTS

Coconut flour is delectable in pancakes, yet quite a challenge to work with. It is extraordinarily absorbent of liquids and requires more eggs and buttermilk than seems imaginable to form a batter that is not too oatmeal-like and crumbly and which will hold together properly when cooking. It is worth the effort, though, as it gives a beautiful sweetly fragrant flavor and a wonderful fluffy texture to pancakes. What's more, coconut flour, made from the pressed coconut "meat," is very high in protein and fiber, and extremely filling. I first came across coconut flour when visiting Canada to see how maple trees are tapped to produce maple syrup. Baked maple apricots make a lovely accompaniment, although fresh nectarines work superbly in summer too.

PREP 20 mins

COOK 30 mins

TOTAL 50 mins

DIETARY

COCONUT FLOUR IS
GLUTEN-FREE

MAKES

12 x 4IN,
SERVES 4

4 large eggs
2 tablespoons coconut oil, melted
1 tablespoon honey
1 teaspoon vanilla extract
½ cup coconut milk
¾ cup buttermilk
½ cup coconut flour
2 teaspoons baking powder
1 teaspoon baking soda
¼ teaspoon salt
2 tablespoons butter, for cooking

FOR THE APRICOTS

12 apricots, halved and pitted
zest of 1 lemon and juice of ½ lemon
6 sprigs of thyme
1 vanilla bean, broken in half
3 tablespoons Canadian maple syrup,
plus extra to serve
1 teaspoon vanilla extract

Preheat the oven to 350°F and butter a large baking dish.

To make the apricots, put them cut-side up in the prepared dish. Sprinkle with the lemon zest and juice, add 2 tablespoons water, and tuck in the thyme and vanilla bean. Mix the maple syrup with the vanilla extract and drizzle over the apricots. Bake for 15 to 20 minutes until tender. Remove from the oven and turn the oven off. Put a plate in the oven to keep the pancakes warm while you make them.

Meanwhile, put the eggs in a bowl and add the coconut oil, honey, and vanilla extract. Mix together well. Stir in the coconut milk and buttermilk. In another bowl, mix together the coconut flour, baking powder, baking soda, and salt. Add the egg mixture to the dry ingredients, stirring gently. The batter will be thick and fluffy.

Melt a little butter in a large nonstick heavy frying pan over medium heat. Add 2 tablespoons of batter for each pancake and flatten slightly. Cook as many pancakes as will fit at one time. Cook for 2 minutes or until the underneath is lightly golden (check by using a spatula, as the batter won't bubble). Flip over carefully and cook for another 1 to 2 minutes until golden. Keep the pancakes warm, and repeat with the remaining batter, adding more butter to the pan as necessary. Serve warm with the apricots and extra maple syrup for added indulgence.

Pannukakku Finnish Pancake

An unusual pancake with real wow factor, this Finnish *pannukakku* is baked in the oven and puffs up as dramatically as a soufflé. It has a delectable custardy interior and a crisp crust and is in essence rather like a French clafoutis. Traditionally, it is served with a rhubarb and strawberry compote, providing an excitingly different flavor combination that mixes tart and sweet. The compote works deliciously with the pancake, which must be served at once. Although the compote is usually served cold, I find it is just as scrumptious warm. This pancake is really easy to put together and is an impressive addition to a dinner party.

PREP 20 mins

* plus 1 hour resting

COOK 20 mins

TOTAL 40 mins

DIETARY

USE GLUTEN-FREE ALL-PURPOSE FLOUR

MAKES

1 x 11 IN, SERVES 4, OR 2 HUNGRY PEOPLE!

3 tablespoons butter, melted
1 cup all-purpose flour, sifted
½ teaspoon vanilla extract
2 tablespoons honey
2 large eggs, beaten
1¼ cups low-fat milk

FOR THE COMPOTE
1 pound rhubarb, cut into 1-inch pieces
zest and juice of 1 orange

¼ cup brown sugar
1¼ cups finely sliced strawberries

FOR THE VANILLA CRÈME FRAÎCHE
1 tablespoon vanilla sugar or
1 teaspoon confectioners' sugar
and ½ teaspoon vanilla extract
¾ cup crème fraîche

Preheat the oven to 425°F. Put an 8-inch ovenproof cast-iron frying pan or baking dish in the oven to heat up.

Put 2 tablespoons of the melted butter in a large bowl and add the flour, vanilla, honey, eggs, and milk. Mix together using a hand mixer to make a pouring batter with the consistency of heavy cream. Let stand for 1 hour, as this will make it rise better.

Use the remaining melted butter to coat the heated frying pan, brushing it up the sides. Pour in the batter and put the pan in the hot oven. Cook for 20 to 25 minutes until the batter has dramatically risen, is a little crusty and golden brown at the edges, and looks like a just-set custard in the middle.

Meanwhile, make the compote: Put the rhubarb in a saucepan over medium heat and add the orange juice and brown sugar. Cover the pan. Cook to dissolve the sugar and then bring to a boil. Reduce the heat to low and add the orange zest, then simmer for 6 minutes. Stir gently, then add the strawberries and cook for 2 minutes. The compote can be served warm or cold.

In a small bowl, stir the vanilla sugar, or confectioners' sugar and vanilla extract mixture, into the crème fraîche. Serve the pancake immediately with the compote and vanilla crème fraîche.

Blintzes

With a history dating back to at least the 1800s, blintzes are an essential dish in Ashkenazi Jewish homes throughout Central Europe. The name itself is Yiddish and means "filled pancakes." They are invariably served at Shavuot, an important Jewish festival that marks the giving of the Torah on Mount Sinai and the beginning of the wheat harvest. It is a time when eating dairy is encouraged.

I like *blintzes* all year round as a wonderfully comforting food for breakfast or a delectable dessert. What I particularly relish about these unusually soft crêpes is that their filling reminds me of baked cheesecake. No wonder they are so popular in New York!

I use a mixture of ricotta and cottage cheese for my filling, together with egg yolk, lemon zest, and vanilla for a lighter touch, although traditionally it is a mixture of curd and cream cheese.

I have fond memories of my Hungarian great-grandmother baking a batch of blintzes when we visited her at her cozy flat in west London. Doilies were de rigueur. Her blintzes were always finished with confectioners' sugar and cinnamon, as cookbook writer Claudia Roden suggests. It might seem counterintuitive, but the crêpes are only cooked on one side initially, then, when they are baked or fried, the other side will brown beautifully.

Blintzes are customarily served with applesauce, although in the summer, a fresh cherry sauce, as used here, makes a delicious alternative.

PREP 20 mins

* plus 40 mins resting

COOK 30 mins

TOTAL 50 mins

DIETARY

USE GLUTEN-FREE
ALL-PURPOSE FLOUR

MAKES

8 TO 10 x 10IN
(BEFORE FILLING),
SERVES 4

2 cups all-purpose flour, sifted
1 cup sparkling water
4 large eggs, beaten
3 tablespoons butter, melted
pinch of salt
¼ cup boiling water
3 tablespoons butter, cubed, plus extra for greasing
2½ tablespoons confectioners' sugar, sifted
½ teaspoon ground cinnamon

FOR THE FILLING
1 cup ricotta
1 cup cottage cheese

1 teaspoon vanilla extract
1 large egg yolk
½ cup confectioners' sugar
zest of 1 lemon

FOR THE CHERRY SAUCE
2½ cups fresh cherries, halved and pitted
zest and juice of 2 oranges
3 tablespoons superfine sugar
1 teaspoon ground cinnamon
3 tablespoons dark rum

In a large bowl, whisk together the flour and sparkling water. Add the eggs, butter, and salt. Whisk again until fully incorporated. The batter should have the consistency of heavy cream. Set aside to rest for at least 10 minutes.

Meanwhile, to make the filling, put the cheeses in a large bowl or in a food processor and add the vanilla extract, egg yolk, and confectioners' sugar. Mix together, then put in the fridge for 30 minutes to firm up.

To make the cherry sauce, put the pitted cherries in a small pan with the orange zest and juice, sugar, cinnamon, and rum. Heat gently to dissolve the sugar. Keep the sauce warm.

Before cooking the crêpes, add ¼ cup boiling water to the batter and whisk thoroughly. This ensures the *blintzes* are soft and pliable when rolling (it's a tip I picked up from chef Michael Zee).

You can bake or fry your blintzes to finish them, although I prefer them baked. If baking, preheat the oven to 350°F and butter a baking dish. To pan-fry, preheat a nonstick frying pan. Test that it is hot enough by putting a few drops of water in the pan. If the water sizzles, it is perfect for cooking the crêpes. If bubbles burst, reduce the heat a little. Wipe the pan with a buttered piece of paper towel, then pour in sufficient batter to coat the pan thinly. Cook over medium heat until the blintz is a little crispy around the edges and firm on top. Do not flip. Stack on a plate interleaved with paper towels. Repeat with the remaining batter, adding more butter to the pan each time. (This can be done ahead of assembling the next stage, if you like.)

When ready to serve, fill the blintzes. Put a blintz on a flat surface cooked-side up. Put 2 to 3 tablespoons of cheese filling in the lower third of the blintz and flatten with the base of a spoon. Be sure not to overfill. Fold the base of the blintz over the filling and then fold the two sides into the middle and roll the blintz from the base to the top.

Put all the rolled blintz in the prepared baking dish. Scatter with cubes of butter. Bake for 15 minutes or until enticingly brown. Alternatively, the assembled blintzes can be fried in a large frying pan in melted butter for 4-5 minutes until crisp and golden, turning once.

Mix the confectioners' sugar with the cinnamon and use to dust the cooked blintzes. Serve immediately with the warm cherry sauce. Traditionally, sour cream is served too, but I think it might be too much, as the blintzes are plenty rich enough.

Crêpes Suzette

A timeless decadent dessert, Crêpes Suzette always creates theater when served. The first time I had them dished up with all due pomp and ceremony was at a dinner dance at The Ritz where they have been serving the dessert since 1906. It is wonderful to behold: an elegant trolley wheeled to the table and the crêpes impeccably made by waiters with white gloves. They certainly know how to flambé!

To modernize the dish, I've made a Suzette butter using a touch of yuzu juice for added zing.

The history of Crêpes Suzette allegedly dates back to an endearing accident in 1895, although Larousse Gastronomique disputes this story. Edward, Prince of Wales—the son of Queen Victoria and the future King Edward VII—was entertaining some gentleman friends and one of their French daughters at the Café de Paris in Monte Carlo. They ordered pancakes for dessert, which were already prepared in the kitchen and the orange sauce with liqueur finished at the table by a young waiter called Henri Charpentier (who went on to become a revered chef). The chafing dish accidentally caught fire, but the flambé accident made the dish taste even better. Edward asked for the dish to be named after Suzette, his friend's young daughter.

I recently tried a rather different flambéed crêpe served with roasted pineapple in a caramel sauce with pomegranate seeds, mint, and rum. This was also served at the table with all due ceremony cooked on a walnut-wood crêpe-making trolley.

PREP 30 mins
plus 1 hour resting

COOK 15 mins

TOTAL 45 mins

DIETARY

USE GLUTEN-FREE FLOUR, USE ALMOND OR SOY MILK

MAKES

12 x 10IN, SERVES 4 TO 6

1⅓ cups all-purpose flour, sifted
3 tablespoons sugar
zest of 1 orange
seeds from 1 vanilla bean
pinch of salt
2 cups whole milk, or soy milk or almond milk
3 large eggs
5 tablespoons butter, melted, plus extra for cooking
5 tablespoons Grand Marnier or Cointreau
4 blood oranges or other oranges

FOR THE SUZETTE BUTTER
½ cup superfine sugar
zest of ½ orange and ½ lime
3 tablespoons yuzu or lime juice
10 tablespoons butter (1 stick + 2 tablespoons), softened
1 tablespoons Grand Marnier or Cointreau

Put the flour in a large bowl and add the sugar, orange zest, vanilla seeds, and salt. Combine well, then make a well in the center.

In a separate bowl, whisk the milk, eggs, and melted butter. Gradually add to the flour mixture, whisking until very smooth. Whisk in the liqueur, then transfer the batter to a glass measuring cup. Cover and set aside at room temperature to rest for 1 hour.

Meanwhile, make the Suzette butter: Put the sugar in a bowl and add the orange and lime zests and the yuzu juice. Stir to dissolve the sugar, then beat in the butter and stir in the liqueur. Set aside.

For the orange slices, use a sharp knife to cut a thin slice of peel and pith from each end of an orange. Put cut-side down on a plate and cut off the rest of the peel and pith. Remove any remaining pith. Cut the flesh into slices, then repeat with the other oranges. Set aside.

Heat a crêpe pan over medium to high heat and, using a heatproof pastry brush, brush with melted butter, then pour in enough batter to evenly yet thinly cover the base of the pan. Cook for 1 to 2 minutes until lightly golden underneath and bubbles appear on the surface. Flip over and cook for 1 minute. Wipe out the pan with paper towels and repeat with the remaining batter, adding more butter to the pan as before. Stack the crêpes as they cook and cover with foil.

To serve, fold the crêpes into quarters. Melt a third of the Suzette butter in a large frying pan over medium heat, then add as many folded crêpes as will fit in the pan. Cook for 30 seconds to coat and reheat, then transfer the crêpes to a warmed heatproof dish or dutch oven. Add the orange slices. Repeat with the remaining crêpes, adding a little more Suzette butter each time. Add any remaining Suzette butter to the pan, bring to a simmer, and cook to a syrup consistency, then pour a little more over the crêpes and put any remaining butter in a container to serve alongside the crêpes.

Return the pan to the heat and add the liqueur to heat. Carefully ignite with a long match, tilting the pan away from you. Be warned, the alcohol should burst into flames. Pour the flaming liqueur over the crêpes. Serve them warm with the orange slices and any remaining Suzette butter to pour over.

Lemon Crunch Pancakes

These pancakes, with a classic lemon and sugar topping, are an all-around favorite. I will often put melted butter in my pancake batter, making it, strictly speaking, a crêpe mix, but in this instance I prefer to keep my pancakes plainer and crisper and merely cook them in butter. Somehow, it makes a better foil for all the tart lemon juice and crunchy sugar (granulated is a must). Definitely experiment with coconut sugar if you can get some, as it adds a delectable, rich note. Adding an extra egg yolk to the batter is also good for enhancing its flavor. Even if you don't usually rest your batter, a mere 30 minutes makes a difference, as it helps the starch in the flour to absorb the liquid and allows the air bubbles from whisking to disperse. I cook my pancakes over a fairly brisk heat, because I like them as thin and crisp as possible with lacy edges, although turn the heat lower if you want a softer, paler "French" finish. If you're selflessly making a batch for family and friends, it is the chef's perk to surreptitiously enjoy the first pancake, straight out of the pan, eaten with one's fingers, drenched in sugar and a squirt of lemon.

PREP *10 mins*

* plus 30 mins resting

COOK *15 mins*

TOTAL *25 mins*

DIETARY

USE GLUTEN-FREE FLOUR

MAKES

12 x 10IN, SERVES 4

1 cup all-purpose flour
pinch of salt
1 large egg, plus 1 yolk
1 cup low-fat milk
butter, for cooking

TO SERVE
bowl of granulated sugar
zest of 1 lemon and the juice of
2 lemons

Sift the flour and salt into a large mixing bowl. Make a well in the center and pour the egg and yolk into it. Mix the milk with 3 tablespoons water and then pour about a quarter of the milk mixture into the flour.

Start whisking the egg and milk together from the center, gradually drawing the flour into the batter until it is all incorporated and you have a smooth mixture with the consistency of heavy cream. Whisk in the remaining milk until the batter is more like half-and-half. Cover and chill in the fridge for at least 30 minutes.

Heat a crêpe pan over medium–high heat. Add a pat of butter and wipe out any excess using paper towels. The batter should sizzle when it hits the pan. Pour a small ladleful of batter into the pan and swirl it around so that the batter spreads out into a thin coat.

Pour any excess batter that doesn't set immediately back into the bowl. When the pancake begins to set and look lacy around the edges, loosen the edges with a spatula and flip it over using the spatula. Alternatively, toss the pancake with swagger. The best way to do this is to loosen the pancake with a spatula, hold the crêpe pan handle with both hands, then jerk the pan upward and slightly forward so that the pancake spins, then be sure to move the pan back to catch the pancake. Make sure the pancake is lying flat across the pan with no folds, then cook for 30 seconds or until lightly golden.

I like to serve my pancakes with a bowl of granulated sugar that has lemon zest grated in it along with lemon juice for guests to serve themselves.

Necci

A delicious fall snack, *necci* is a dish typical of the Tuscan region of the Garfagnana, a mountainous area near Lucca in Italy that is covered in chestnut forests. Traditionally, *necci* are made over an open fire and cooked between a pair of *testi*, cast iron pans that have a long handle like a pizza paddle, which are turned to cook both sides of the *necci*. The pans can still be found for sale in Tuscany. Going further back still, *necci* were made by heating up flat terracotta dishes over an open fire. Once hot, they were covered with chestnut leaves before the necci batter was spread on them. Then another layer of chestnut leaves was used to cover the batter, and another stone dish used to cover the mixture. As well as adding to the flavor of the *necci*, the leaves left a leaf imprint on them too. My method is somewhat more straightforward. *Necci* are eaten warm with a dollop of fresh sheep's milk ricotta cheese and a drizzle of chestnut honey. For a special occasion, add some marron glacé for utter chestnut indulgence. For a savory *necci*, cook some pancetta to serve with the ricotta.

PREP 10 mins
plus resting time

COOK 20 mins

TOTAL 30 mins

DIETARY

CHESTNUT FLOUR IS
GLUTEN-FREE

MAKES

12 X 10IN,
SERVES 4 TO 6

2 cups chestnut flour
2 tablespoons extra virgin olive oil,
plus extra for cooking
pinch of salt

2 marron glacé (optional), chopped
1⅔ cups sheep's milk ricotta
chestnut honey, to serve

Preheat the oven to 225°F and warm a plate to keep the pancakes warm while you make them. In a large bowl, mix the flour with enough water to get a smooth, dense batter slightly thicker than a usual crêpe batter; you will need about 1¼ cups water.

Add the olive oil and salt and mix again. Lightly oil a frying pan over medium heat.

Add 2 spoonfuls of the batter to the pan and tilt it slightly to coat the pan evenly (note that this batter does not move as fluidly as a crêpe batter). Cook for 2 minutes or until you see that the top of the batter looks dry. Loosen with a spatula, flip over, and cook for 1 minute. Keep the pancakes warm and repeat with the remaining batter, adding more oil to the pan as necessary.

When all the *necci* are ready, add the marron glacé, if using, to the ricotta, then spread some over each *necci*. Fold them in two, or roll them up and serve them drizzled with chestnut honey.

Kaiserschmarrn

An unusual, almost soufflé-like fluffy caramelized pancake, *kaiserschmarrn* is served shredded with plum compote. It is a dessert popular in Austria, southern Germany, Slovenia, and northern Croatia. *Kaiserschmarrn* translates colloquially as "the Emperor's mess" and gets its name from Kaiser Franz Josef I. As ever, there are various apocryphal stories associated with this dish, including one about the ever-so-fussy Empress Elizabeth who was always watching her waistline, so the Kaiser ordered the pancake to be cut up to look less daunting on the plate. I convince myself it is less fattening because it is in little shreds! However, she still decided not to eat it, so the Kaiser, finding it totally addictive, devoured the lot. Another story has the Kaiser on tour and stopping at a farmer's home in the Alps for lunch. The farmer got so flustered that he messed up the pancake and cut it into bits to cover his mistakes and smothered it with plum jam. It is the perfect pancake for a messy cook. The sweet batter with whisked egg whites, making it ethereally light, is usually made with rum-soaked raisins, although I found it tastier with barberries soaked in port for an unusual and slightly tart contemporary Ottoman twist to the recipe. The pancake is split up with two forks into pieces and finished in butter to make it crisp and completely irresistible. It is traditional to finish the *kaiserschmarrn* with an alpine avalanche of confectioners' sugar on top.

PREP *15 mins*

* *plus 30 mins soaking*

COOK *15 mins*

TOTAL *30 mins*

DIETARY

USE GLUTEN-FREE
ALL-PURPOSE FLOUR

MAKES

2 x 10IN,
SERVES 4

⅓ cup barberries or raisins
2 tablespoons port or dark rum
4 large egg yolks
¼ cup superfine sugar
pinch of salt
2 cups low-fat milk
½ teaspoon vanilla extract
1¼ cups all-purpose flour, sifted
5 large egg whites
4 tablespoons butter
confectioners' sugar, to serve

FOR THE VANILLA AND CINNAMON
PLUM COMPOTE
½ cup brown sugar
1 pound plums, pitted and cut into
quarters
seeds from 1 vanilla bean
1 cinnamon stick
1¼ cups heavy whipping cream
1 teaspoon vanilla extract

Preheat the oven to 225°F and warm a baking sheet lined with parchment paper to keep the pancakes warm while you make them. Put the barberries or raisins and port in a bowl to macerate for 30 minutes. Drain and dry on paper towels.

Meanwhile, to make the compote, put ¾ cup of cold water into a large pan over medium–high heat and add the sugar. Bring to a boil to dissolve the sugar, then let the mixture bubble for 30 seconds.

Add the plums, vanilla seeds, and cinnamon stick and simmer for 8 to 10 minutes. Transfer the plums to a bowl and simmer the sauce so that it reduces and thickens. Pour over the plums and let cool slightly. Set aside.

Put the whipping cream in a bowl. Add the vanilla extract, then whip with a hand mixer until thick. Set aside.

Put the egg yolks in a bowl and whisk in the sugar and salt until pale yellow and thick. Stir in the milk and vanilla extract, then gradually and gently stir in the flour. Finally, add the barberries.

Just before cooking, put the egg whites into a clean bowl and whisk until they form stiff peaks. Fold into the pancake batter using a metal spoon.

Heat 1 tablespoon of the butter over low heat in a deep, heavy frying pan and pour in half the batter to a depth of 2 inches. Cook for 3 minutes or until the batter has risen, the top is beginning to set, and the underneath is lightly brown. Slide out of the pan and transfer to a plate. Melt another tablespoon of the butter around the pan. Using oven mitts, carefully invert the pan over the plate and flip to return the pancake to the pan. Cook the other side for 2 to 3 minutes until just set.

Using two forks, break the finished pancake into six to eight pieces and put on the preheated baking sheet. Keep the pancake warm and repeat with the remaining batter, adding more butter to the pan as before. Break up the second pancake as before.

Heat the remaining butter over medium heat and cook the pancake pieces for 2 minutes, turning to crisp the ripped edges. Pile them on a plate and drench generously with confectioners' sugar. Serve with the plum compote and whipped vanilla cream.

Layered Crêpe Cake

WITH CHOCOLATE RUM GANACHE AND PRALINE CREAM

Crêpes, chocolate, nuts, rum, and cream—this celebration cake really has it all. It's creamy, moist, rich, and sophisticated with plenty of interesting texture in each bite. A small slice suffices, although the greedy will ask for seconds. Make the crêpes as thin as you dare. The French might call it a mille-feuille crêpe gateau, although aiming for a 20-layer cake is ambitious enough. The cake definitely improves if kept chilled in the fridge overnight, so it is perfect to make ahead for a special occasion. A great friend who used to be a pastry chef gave me an insider's insight into how to make praline like a pro.

PREP 60 mins

* plus 1 hour resting & chilling

COOK 20 mins

TOTAL 80 mins

DIETARY

USE GLUTEN-FREE
ALL-PURPOSE FLOUR

MAKES

1 X 10IN CAKE,
SERVES 8

2¾ cups all-purpose flour
⅓ cup good-quality cocoa powder
pinch of salt
2 tablespoons superfine sugar
3¾ cups low-fat milk
3 tablespoons melted butter, plus extra
for cooking
strawberries or cherries in rum or
kirsch, to serve

FOR THE PRALINE CREAM
½ cup superfine sugar

½ cup blanched almonds
½ cup blanched hazelnuts
2½ cups heavy cream

FOR THE CHOCOLATE GANACHE
9 ounces good-quality dark chocolate
(70% cocoa solids), broken
1 cup heavy cream
3 tablespoons superfine sugar
¼ cup espresso
2 tablespoons dark rum

Sift the flour, cocoa powder, and salt into a large mixing bowl and stir in the sugar. Gradually whisk in the milk using a hand mixer (the batter should be the consistency of half-and-half). Add the butter and whisk again. Set the batter aside to rest for 30 minutes at room temperature. Pour into a glass measuring cup.

To make the praline, pour the sugar into a pan. Add 3 tablespoons water and set the pan over medium–low heat to allow the sugar to dissolve slowly, stirring. Bring to a boil and continue to cook until the syrup turns a pale amber color. Working quickly, pour the almonds and hazelnuts into the pan and continue to cook for 1 minute or until the caramel turns a deeper amber and the nuts are a little toasted. Pour the praline onto a baking sheet and leave until completely cold and hardened. Break the praline into chunks. Put into a small plastic bag and secure it. Bash with a rolling pin until coarsely chopped. Alternatively, blitz in a food processor. Whip the cream and add the crushed praline. Set aside.

To make the chocolate ganache, melt the chocolate in a heatproof bowl over a pan of gently simmering water, making sure the base of the bowl doesn't touch the water, and stirring occasionally. In a separate small pan, heat the heavy cream and sugar until it is just about to boil, turn down the heat, then stir in the coffee and rum. Remove from the heat. Combine with the chocolate. Cover and cool, then put in the freezer for at least 30 minutes until it thickens.

Warm a heavy nonstick crêpe pan over medium–high heat. Use a heatproof pastry brush to sparingly cover the pan with melted butter. Use a small cup to pour in equal amounts of batter for each crêpe, using just enough to coat the base of the pan, then swirl it around to spread the batter to the edges. The crêpes should be as thin as possible. Pour any excess batter back into the cup and then into the mixing bowl.

Cook each crêpe for 1 minute or until it is just beginning to get a little crisp at the edges. Flip over and cook for a another 40 to 60 seconds. Stack the cooked crêpes on a plate—there is no need to separate them with wax paper. Add a little extra milk if the first crêpes are too thick, and, if the crêpes are not cooking evenly, reduce the heat a little. Repeat with the remaining batter, adding more butter to the pan as necessary. Aim to make about at least 12 crêpes.

Put the first crêpe on a serving plate and spread it with a thin layer of chocolate ganache. Add a second crêpe and spread it with a slightly thicker layer of praline cream. Repeat, alternating the layers until all the crêpes and the praline cream and chocolate ganache are used up. Chill the pancake gateau in the fridge for at least 1 hour or preferably overnight before serving.

I serve it with strawberries on the side in summer, or cherries in rum or kirsch would be fabulous for the winter. For added extravagance, an extra bowl of half-and-half on the side could be proffered, although this is probably an indulgence too far!

Walnut and Raisin Palatschinken

WITH CHOCOLATE SAUCE

This decadent dessert crêpe was invented by Károly Gundel of the world-famous grand Budapest Gundel restaurant overlooking the City Park in Hungary. At Gundel, the pancakes are flambéed with rum at the table, although I prefer to merely add dark rum to the nut filling, which I serve more coarsely chopped than the traditional paste, as I find this more flavorful.

PREP 25 mins

★ plus 30 mins resting

COOK 15 mins

TOTAL 40 mins

DIETARY

USE GLUTEN-FREE ALL-PURPOSE FLOUR

MAKES

8 X 10IN, SERVES 4

2 cups all-purpose flour, sifted
2 tablespoons superfine sugar
2 large eggs, beaten
1 tablespoon melted butter, plus extra butter for cooking
1½ cups low-fat milk

FOR THE FILLING
1 cup walnuts, toasted in a frying pan and coarsely chopped
⅓ cup raisins
zest of 1 lemon

⅓ cup superfine sugar
¼ cup dark rum

FOR THE CHOCOLATE SAUCE
9 ounces plain chocolate, broken into small pieces
½ cup whipping cream
1 large egg yolk
¼ cup corn syrup
a pat of butter
pinch of salt

Preheat the oven to 225°F and heat a plate to keep the pancakes warm while you make them. Put the flour in a bowl and stir in the sugar. Add the eggs and melted butter, then gradually incorporate the milk, whisking constantly and making sure to incorporate all the flour. Set aside to rest for at least 30 minutes. Transfer to a glass measuring cup.

Meanwhile, to make the filling, put the walnuts in a bowl and add the raisins, lemon zest, sugar, and rum. Mix together, then set aside.

To make the chocolate sauce, put the chocolate and cream in a small heavy-bottomed saucepan over low heat. Heat, stirring occasionally, until the chocolate has melted into the cream to make a smooth paste. Stir in the egg yolk, followed by the corn syrup, butter, and salt to give a glossy sauce. Keep warm over very low heat.

Heat a frying pan over medium heat and add a little butter. Spread evenly with paper towels, removing any excess. Pour in enough batter to cover the pan very sparsely, as *palatschinken* should be ultra-thin. Cook for 1 to 2 minutes until the underneath is lightly golden and starting to crisp at the edges. Flip over and cook for 1 minute or until lightly golden. Keep the pancakes warm and repeat with the remaining batter to make eight *palatschinken*, adding more butter to the pan as necessary.

To serve, put 1 to 2 tablespoons of the walnut filling onto each crêpe, roll it up, and pour over the warm chocolate sauce.

Atayef (Kataif) Arabic Pancake

The gorgeous dessert-like pancake, *atayef*, takes a little practice to get right, but is worth it. The batter needs to be thinner than half-and-half to perfect the requisite bubbly, filigree-like texture, yet still be able to hold its delectable filling. The *atayef* are cooked for a mere minute to turn pale golden on one side only. The other side is velvety because it is covered with bubbles that allow the flavors of the filling to permeate the *atayef*.

PREP 20 mins

COOK 20 mins

TOTAL 40 mins

DIETARY

VEGAN

MAKES

30 x 4IN,
SERVES 6 TO 8

1 cup flour
⅓ cup semolina
½ teaspoon fast-acting yeast
1 teaspoon baking powder, plus extra
if needed
2 tablespoons superfine sugar
2 tablespoons peanut oil
2 tablespoons orange blossom water

FOR THE FILLING
⅔ cup blanched almonds
1 teaspoon ground cinnamon
1 teaspoon cardamom seeds, crushed
1 tablespoon light brown sugar
1 tablespoon orange blossom water
9-ounce container clotted cream or
crème fraîche

Put the flour in a large bowl and add the semolina, yeast, baking powder, and sugar, then whisk to mix well. Add the oil, orange blossom water, and 1¾ cups warm water, whisking until you get a thin, well-combined mixture the consistency of half-and-half. Set aside to rest for 30 minutes. Meanwhile, preheat the oven to 400°F.

To make the filling, put the almonds on a baking sheet and roast for 10 minutes. Let cool. Put the cooled almonds in a plastic bag, seal, and crush with a rolling pin. Pour into a bowl and add the cinnamon, cardamom seeds, and sugar. Set aside.

Heat a large nonstick frying pan over medium heat. Pour 1 tablespoon of the batter to make small *atayef*. The batter should start to bubble at the sides immediately and spread across the whole surface. If this doesn't happen, the batter is not thin enough, in which case gradually whisk in an additional ¼ cup warm water and try again. If there are still not enough bubbles, add another 1 teaspoon baking powder, whisk, and try again. Cook as many pancakes as will fit at one time. Cook for 1 minute—the surface should still be velvety and smooth and lightly golden underneath.

The pancake is only cooked on one side and not flipped. Transfer the *atayef* to a clean kitchen towel and fold the kitchen towel over to cover and stop the *atayef* from drying out. The *atayef* are stacked bubbly sides together. This is important, as it will soften them, making them easier to stuff and seal, and it will prevent them from splitting. Repeat with the remaining batter. (They can be stored stacked bubbly sides together in tightly sealed plastic bags for a few hours, if necessary.)

When the *atayef* are cool, fill them. Stir the orange blossom water into the cream. To fill the *atayef*, fold the *atayef* at one end only and pinch the sides as if making a tiny bouquet. Fill with orange blossom-scented cream or crème fraîche and top with the nut mixture.

Pang Jee

THAI COCONUT AND BANANA PANCAKES

I find the combination of coconut and banana irresistible, especially when mixed with the butterscotch richness of palm sugar and the chewy texture of glutinous rice flour. I remember tasting *pang jee* many years ago at a food stall along Lumpini Park in Bangkok. There was such a huge line that I naturally had to join to find out what was so incredibly popular. The *pang jee* were being made at great speed by a very smiley wizened elderly Thai woman in a vivid yellow silk dress. They are delicious served warm as a dessert with vanilla ice cream or as an afternoon snack with jasmine tea.

PREP 15 mins
plus cooling

COOK 15 mins

TOTAL 30 mins

DIETARY

GLUTEN-FREE

MAKES

18 x 3IN,
SERVES 6

⅔ cup coconut cream
3 tablespoons palm sugar
1 banana or 2 namwa (small ultra-sweet bananas, often available frozen)
⅓ cup glutinous rice flour

⅔ cup shredded coconut, unsweetened
⅔ cup fresh coconut chunks, if available, finely chopped
pinch of salt

Put the coconut cream in a small pan over low heat and add the palm sugar. Stir until the sugar has dissolved. Remove from the heat and let cool.

In a mixing bowl, mash the banana. Add the rice flour, shredded coconut, fresh coconut, salt, and the coconut-cream mixture. Stir until well-combined—it will be a very thick batter.

Heat a nonstick frying pan over medium–low heat. No oil is required. Drop tablespoonfuls of batter onto the pan into a round shape about 1¼ inches wide. Cook as many pancakes as will fit at one time. Cook for 1 to 2 minutes until the bottom is golden. Flip over and press down slightly, then cook for another 1 to 2 minutes or until golden. Cool slightly on a wire rack.

Pang jee are best served warm, but they are delicious at room temperature too.

Baked Caramelized Apple Pancake

This traditional German pancake made with caramelized apple slices flavored with cinnamon then topped with a sweet batter reminds me of a tarte tatin's gorgeous indulgence. I like to add a little calvados or kirsch to the batter to amp it up. Since it's cooked in a very hot oven, the eggy batter bubbles and puffs up dramatically, so serve it at once to enjoy the full impact. Nutmeg ice cream or the brown-sugar whipped cream used here complements it beautifully. Confusingly, these pancakes are often referred to as "Dutch babies" in the US and Canada. They've recently become an Instagram obsession. The name was supposedly coined in the early 1900s by the daughter of the owner of Manca's Café, a family-run restaurant in Seattle. The café no longer exists, yet the name lives on. The "Dutch" refers to the group of German–American immigrants known as the Pennsylvania Dutch, although "Dutch" is understood to be a corruption of Deutsch. Savory Dutch babies filled with goat cheese and parmesan, but rosemary and thyme are great too.

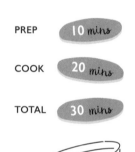

PREP 10 mins

COOK 20 mins

TOTAL 30 mins

DIETARY

USE GLUTEN-FREE
ALL-PURPOSE FLOUR

MAKES

1 x 10IN,
SERVES 4

3 tablespoons butter

4 large sweet apples, peeled, cored, and sliced

¼ cup brown sugar, plus

2 tablespoons extra

1 teaspoon ground cinnamon

1 cup all-purpose flour, sifted

3 tablespoons superfine sugar

¼ teaspoon salt

¾ cup low-fat milk

¼ cup Greek yogurt

3 large eggs, beaten

1 teaspoon vanilla extract

2 tablespoon calvados or kirsch (optional)

1¼ cups heavy whipping cream

Preheat the oven to 450°F.

Melt the butter in a large 10-inch ovenproof, nonstick frying pan over medium heat. Add the sliced apples and sprinkle with the ¼ cup brown sugar and the cinnamon. Cook the apples gently for 8 to 10 minutes until just starting to soften and caramelize, then transfer the apple to a plate. Set aside.

Meanwhile, in a large bowl, mix the flour, sugar, and salt. In a separate bowl, whisk the milk, yogurt, eggs, vanilla, and calvados, if using. Add to the flour mixture and whisk again to ensure there are no lumps and the batter has the consistency of heavy cream.

Pour the batter over the apples. Put into the hot oven and cook for 15 to 20 minutes until the batter has puffed up, has just started to set in the center, and is turning golden at the edges. While it is cooking, put the whipping cream and the 2 tablespoons brown sugar in a bowl and whip with a hand mixer until the sugar is gently incorporated. Transfer the cream to a serving bowl. When the apple pancake is cooked, immediately turn it out of the pan and serve it cut into wedges with the brown-sugar whipped cream.

Dorayaki

JAPANESE HONEY PANCAKES WITH AZUKI BEAN AND MASCARPONE FILLING

Legend has it that *dorayaki* were first prepared when a samurai named Benkei accidentally left his gong (dora) behind at a farmer's house where he was hiding out. The enterprising farmer used it to cook little "gong cakes," hence the name. Manga comic books have made *dorayaki* extremely popular among children in Japan, especially served sandwiched with Nutella and accompanied by a glass of milk.

PREP 15 mins

COOK 15 mins
plus cooling

TOTAL 30 mins

DIETARY

USE GLUTEN-FREE
ALL-PURPOSE FLOUR

MAKES

8 x 4IN SANDWICHES,
SERVES 4

1 large egg, beaten

1 large egg, separated

1 tablespoon superfine sugar, plus
3 teaspoons

1 tablespoon honey

½ teaspoon vanilla extract

1 tablespoon sunflower or canola oil,
plus extra for cooking

⅓ cup low-fat milk

⅔ cup all-purpose flour, sifted

1 teaspoon baking powder

FOR THE FILLING

3½ ounces adzuki red bean mixture

7 ounces mascarpone

Put the beaten egg and egg yolk in large bowl. Add 1 tablespoon sugar, the honey, vanilla, oil, milk, flour, and baking powder. Mix gently with a whisk, starting from the middle of the bowl and moving outward until all the ingredients are just incorporated and the mixture is foamy and falls in ribbons when the whisk is lifted from the bowl.

Put the egg white in a clean bowl with the remaining sugar and, using a hand mixer, slowly whisk until it forms soft peaks, then increase the speed to form stiff peaks. Add about a third of the egg white to the egg-yolk mixture using a whisk and a very light circular motion. Repeat with the second third of egg white. Now use a spatula to fold in the remaining egg white, ensuring that the mixture remains full of air bubbles and doesn't deflate. If it does, the dorayaki will be flat and rubbery.

Heat a crêpe pan over medium heat, add 1 tablespoon oil, then wipe off any excess with paper towels. The pan should be sufficiently oiled for the dorayaki to cook to an enticing pale golden color, but not so much that they color unevenly. Add 1 generous tablespoon of batter for each dorayaki, and swirl it around quickly to a diameter of about 3 inches. Cook for 1 to 2 minutes until golden. Check to see if it is done by tentatively sliding a spatula underneath. If there are no wet crumbs sticking to the spatula, it is ready to flip over. Cook for 40 to 60 seconds until golden yet still a little soft in the center. Transfer to a wire rack to cool completely. Repeat with the remaining batter, adding more oil to the pan as before.

When the *dorayaki* are cool, put the adzuki mixture in a bowl, add the mascarpone, and combine well. Use 1 heaping tablespoonful to sandwich two similar-sized *dorayaki* together, spreading the filling with a palette knife. If the *dorayaki* are not to be eaten immediately, wrap them in plastic wrap to keep them from drying out. They can also be frozen for up to 1 month.

Index

Acknowledgments

There are so many people I want to thank, I barely know where to start.

An enormous thank you to Kyle Cathie for recognizing the need for a new book dedicated to pancakes around the world that I've long wanted to write. I greatly enjoyed working with such a calm, organized and consultative team whose company has been a huge pleasure, especially Judith Hannam, Sophie Allen, Hannah Coughlin, Victoria Scales, and Julia Barder.

Thank you so much to my agent Martine Carter for all her cajoling, encouragement, and patience.

I am in photographic awe of the astonishingly talented Maja Smend, who has made sure that every pancake looks exquisite and different. Equally, I've been hugely impressed by Lizzie Harris for not only her speedy and ever delicious culinary skills in cooking up my recipes, but her great sense of style, enthusiasm, and fun in ensuring every dish is gorgeous and inspiring. Rosie Mackean, too, for being such an eagle-eyed, quick, and knowledgeable assistant with impeccable Spanish. Thanks to Tonia Shuttleworth for finding so many beautiful and interesting props. I coveted so many of those plates.

I hugely appreciate all the encouragement, love, and help so many friends have given me with bringing the book together and, especially Jo Lamiri for her endless enthusiasm and sharing so much indispensable critical feedback and laughter, especially on late night aebelskiver and wine sessions. Louise Simpson for masses of support, particularly on blintz making and taking over her kitchen. Helen Mangham, one of my oldest and best friends, whom I once shared a kitchen with in those heady post-college days, for indulging my pancake making and research over a wonderful, fun stay at her home in France. Huge, huge thanks to Philip Owens of Bespoke Menu Design, a dear friend and enormous creative culinary influence on me. Helen Hokin for being so excited about the book and her indispensable feedback and creative marketing insight. Vivienne Huang and Loretta Liu for their generous input on some of my Asian recipes. Romy Gill, for kindly helping me with an easy dosa recipe. Food writers, including Jill Norman, Diana Henry, Jenny Linford, Catherine Phipps, and Sabrina Ghayour for their much appreciated advice and insight. Mary Craig for her intelligent and incisive critical input. My wonderful neighbor Serena Rowe for so much enthusiasm, fun, and being a great taster for impromptu dinner parties. Deep thanks to Francis Pigott, with whom I discovered Hampstead's creperie kiosk long ago, and our gorgeous, memorable vacation in Brittany involving so many galettes. My big-hearted, generous parents for giving me such a strong food background and for embracing so many tastings, remembering pancakes past, and giving so much love and support. I promise I will make you atayif again!

Thanks to Sous Chef, a brilliant resource for the more recondite ingredients, Billington's and Shipton Mill for their great products, Lakeland, Greenpan, and Borough Kitchen for indispensable kitchen equipment.

And finally, not least, to my son Theo for always been enthusiastic and giving creative feedback when it was pancakes yet again for supper.